PRAISE FOR *UNDERSTANDING ST. PAUL*

Many books have been written over the centuries concerning the letters of St. Paul. Yet I find this book, *Understanding St Paul, A Concise Guide to St. Paul, his Theology and Letters.* to be a compilation of a wealth of historical, cultural, biblical and spiritual material which presents St. Paul in a very clear and unique way. I am honored to have been asked to review this book and I highly recommend it for your edification and inspiration.

—*Most Rev. Eduardo A. Nevares,*
Auxiliary Bishop of Phoenix

After years of extensive study, teaching, preaching, and living the Gospels, Deacon Bob Evans has composed this excellent, thought-provoking commentary on the letters of St. Paul. This concise guide assists the reader in appreciating Paul's resolute, life-long effort to lead us to a personal relationship with Jesus Christ. St. Paul and his recipients had a completely different perception and view of the world from what we share as modern-day westerners. In this book, Deacon Evans brings to us an understanding of the culture and reality of St. Paul's time. We begin to "hear" St. Paul's words and appreciate them in our own hearts and minds. I recommend Deacon Evans' work to all who are serious students of biblical studies consistent with the Magisterial teachings of the Catholic Church.

—*Deacon James Trant,*
Director of the Diaconate,
Diocese of Phoenix

In *Understanding St. Paul, A Concise Guide to St. Paul, his Theology and Letters,* Deacon Bob Evans provides a much-needed resource: a simple, straightforward introduction to the life and work of St. Paul, intended for the common Christian. You will find in these pages both a portrait of, and context for, the greatest Christian evangelist, which will prepare you to read St. Paul's letters with a whole new level of appreciation.

—*Steve Greene, Director,*
Kino Catechetical Institute

The best words to describe what Dcn. Evans accomplishes in this book, *Understanding St. Paul, A Concise Guide to St. Paul, his Theology and Letters,* is concise clarity. By placing the reader in the time, place, and situation of each of Paul's letters, one walks away with enhanced insights into each of these foundational writings. This book is a must read for anyone seeking an accurate understanding of the teachings of nearly half of the books which comprise the New Testament.

—*Deacon Dennis Lambert,*
Catholic author of For Real?
Christ's Presence in the Eucharist
and The Table.

UNDERSTANDING
ST. PAUL

DEACON BOB EVANS

UNDERSTANDING ST. PAUL

A CONCISE GUIDE TO HIS THEOLOGY, HIS LETTERS, AND HIS LIFE

SOPHIA INSTITUTE PRESS
Manchester, New Hampshire

Cover Designer: Updatefordesign Studio

Cover art: *Saint Paul Writing His Epistles* by Valentin de Boulogne

Unless otherwise stated, the Scripture citations used in this work are taken from the *New American Bible, revised edition* © 2010, 1991, 1986, 1970 by the Confraternity of Christian Doctrine. In some places, the author has added italics foe emphasis. Excerpts are from the United States Conference of Catholic Bishops website, www.usccb.org.

Excerpts from the *Catechism of the Catholic Church* are from the second edition for use in the United States of America, © 1994 and 1997, Libreria Editrice Vaticana.

Excerpts from Vatican documents are from the Vatican website, www.vatican.va.

Nihil Obstat:
Fr. Eugene Mary of the Trinity, Erem. Dio., STL
Censor Deputatus

Imprimatur:
✠ Thomas J. Olmsted
Bishop of Phoenix
April 8, 2022

Sophia Institute Press
Box 5284, Manchester, NH 03108
1-800-888-9344
www.SophiaInstitute.com

Sophia Institute Press is a registered trademark of Sophia Institute.

paperback ISBN 978-1-64413-814-4

ebook ISBN 978-1-64413-815-1

Library of Congress Control Number: 2022949376

First printing

DEDICATION

*To Fr. Kilian McCaffrey, who, as a seminarian in our parish,
first ignited my interest in knowing St. Paul better;
and to Fr. Pat Robinson, who served as my
supportive and encouraging pastor for many years.*

CONTENTS

PREFACE

He is no fool who gives up what he cannot keep,
to gain what he cannot lose.

Jim Elliott, missionary
martyred January 8, 1956

St. Paul was among the first Christians to proclaim the "good news" of Jesus Christ in written form. He did so by responding to the issues and concerns in communities where he ministered, which faced both periods of relative calm and periods of great turmoil. Paul sought to interpret it all in the light of God's plan of salvation. He traveled much of the then-known world, announcing a Church that was not just for the righteous but for all—that is, a universal Church.

His wholehearted acceptance of God's grace in his efforts and his commitment to use that grace fully empowered him. Paul's letters convey a person who was deeply committed to being for others what they needed most. In this great endeavor, he gave us much of the vocabulary we still use today to articulate, for others and ourselves, the life, death, and Resurrection of Jesus Christ.

We learn about Paul from Luke's Acts of the Apostles and from Paul's letters. There are thirteen documents attributed to St. Paul that have survived and that are now part of the New Testament. As we will learn, quite a few scholars contend that some of these letters were not actually written by Paul but by disciples of Paul. In this book, we will touch on some of the arguments for and against Paul's having written those letters. Further, next only to Jesus, Paul has been the most influential figure in the history of Christianity. The range and depth of his thought, and his passionate involvement with those to whom he wrote, have left no Christian unaffected by what Paul wrote. So we should expect that there will be disagreement over the interpretation of certain passages in his letters.

It's important to recognize that the Gospels, which were written in story form, often engender spontaneous attraction, but trying to decipher a number of passages in Paul's letters can be quite daunting for many people. So if you first absorb the material in this brief guide, you are more apt to appreciate Paul, the man who did more than anyone else in history to lead people to see what Jesus Christ means to the world. Also, reread, every now and then, the glossary of terms at the end of this book (it's just a few pages). Remind yourself what those terms meant in the times when Paul was writing. It may be helpful for the reader to have a Bible on hand when reading this book.

You will find that Paul was a man of great intensity who was capable of generating deep friendships. Paul's letters give evidence of extraordinary loyalty. A lasting appreciation of him and his theology flowed from the quills of those who, remaining anonymous, wrote for him and in his name.

Today, there is a vast amount of literature on St. Paul and his writings, and this corpus continues to grow each year. So, one might reasonably ask, why this book? Well, between the many volumes of scholarly works and the even larger number of commentaries on Paul, there appears to be a need for a brief guide, perhaps no more than about a hundred and fifty pages or so, for the many Christians who are not scholarly yet thirst for a better understanding of St. Paul, his theology, and his letters. The purpose of this book, which is intentionally brief, is to fulfill that need, and so I will focus primarily on those passages people find most difficult to understand.

"But there are other brief guides to St. Paul already available; how is this one different?" Let me explain. St. Paul's writings were not theological treatises, but letters. His letters give us one side of a conversation with specific people about specific issues. Both the writer and the recipients shared a common knowledge of those issues, and the writer's words called forth in the minds of his first listeners much that was not explicitly stated in the letters.

The writer and the recipients also had a socially shared understanding of reality. First-century Middle Easterners had perceptions of the world and their relationship to one another that were quite different from those shared by modern-day westerners. Those perceptions shaped many of the issues they confronted, as well as Paul's advice to them. Therefore, if we are to gain insights into the meanings Paul intended, we need to "hear" his words in the cultural context in which they were written. This book is an attempt, by a non-scholar drawing on the work of many scholars, to provide easily understood explanations of Paul's words in the cultural context of his times. (See the bibliography section of this book for a complete list of the sources and references for the material presented in this book.)

There will be those who may disagree with some of the conclusions or interpretations offered in this book; that's to be expected. Biblical studies is not an exact science; and people come to Scripture from many different perspectives. I am an ordained deacon in the Roman Catholic Church. As such, I sought in this book to adhere to the principles of biblical studies set out in the *Catechism of the Catholic Church* (*CCC*). The conclusions and interpretations in this book are consistent with the teachings of the Catholic Church.

This text was derived from a series of classes that I led at Blessed Sacrament Roman Catholic Parish in Scottsdale, Arizona, from March 29 through May 3, 2021. I have incorporated many of the questions raised in those classes. And I thank the many who attended the sessions, week after week. They were deeply invested in hearing more clearly St. Paul's words. Many of the handouts from those classes have been blended into the material covered in this book. My special thanks go to our pastor, Fr. Bryan Buenger, whose support for biblical studies at the parish level has blossomed into a number of Bible study series.

Deacon Bob Evans
January 2022

FOREWORD

Although, not one of the original twelve Apostles of Jesus, St Paul was without a doubt, one of the most prolific contributors to the New Testament. He wrote his Letters to meet ordinary problems encountered by the Church to refute false doctrines, to strengthen the ethical implications of the Gospel message, to share in the common catechetical and moral materials, and giving encouragement in the face of the delay of the Parousia.

Paul's letters expand the gospel message because he was converted and called as a "witness to the gentiles" by the resurrected Christ. While Paul (Saul) was persecuting the early church, he certainly heard the stories of Jesus' life, death and resurrection, but he never knew the man.

The letters of Paul are so relevant today. The issues he addressed in his letters two thousand years ago are very much present in our time. His letters addressed issues as they relate to politics, the question of ethnicity and equality. These issues still rear their ugly heads in our age and time. At face value, Paul's letters appear easy to read. But they are actually quite difficult to interpret.

Deacon Bob Evans, with great scholarly touch has helped to "simplify" St Paul and made our reading of him easy. The book in your hands, *Understanding St Paul, A Concise Guide to His Theology and His Life*, provides all the answers you need for better appreciation of St Paul's subject matter while penning down these letters. In fifteen chapters, Deacon Bob provides context for which the reader is better positioned to situate the different themes as they appear in the letters.

This book is the best I have read that speaks to the thorny issues as presented in the Pauline letters. It is therefore my honor to recommend this book to all those who seek to penetrate the mind of St Paul either for intellectual, leisure or spiritual purposes.

Rev. Williams Kaura Abba
Academic Dean, St, Albert Institute
Diocese of Kafanchan, Nigeria

ONE

✠ ✠ ✠

AN INTRODUCTION TO ST. PAUL

1.1 PAUL'S STYLE OF COMMUNICATION

There is a treasure trove of insights in St. Paul's letters—insights into the life, death, and Resurrection of Jesus Christ and how to live out the life of self-emptying to which Jesus calls each of us. There are also many insights into Paul himself—how he came to better understand Jesus' mission over a period of years and how the culture of his times shaped his articulation of that mission—and into the early struggles of Christ's followers, both among themselves and with the world around them.

Through most of his missionary life, Paul wrestled with questions of "Why?" Why did God come into the world as a human being? Why did He have to suffer so greatly? Why is keeping the Commandments necessary if we are unable to earn our salvation? Why, why, why? Formulating adequate answers to these questions was central to Paul's life, for his own well-being, for that of those he served, and to respond to his principal opponents: other Jews.

For many people, their favorite Bible verses are from Paul's letters. We draw much inspiration and encouragement from them. But many also find portions of Paul's letters very difficult to understand, sometimes even puzzling. This brief guide is intended to enable a deeper understanding of Paul's letters, and the messages contained therein, by "breaking open" many of those poorly understood areas and many of those passages in which there are conflicting interpretations or even considerable controversy.

We should begin by recognizing that Paul's letters addressed specific community issues, not principally theological issues. And so Paul's letters do not provide neat, cogent answers to the "why" questions. He was not making theological presentations when he wrote. So we have to draw from here and there throughout his letters to bring together the answers. Consequently, having a satisfactory understanding of St. Paul, his theology, and his letters is something that has escaped many Christians.

Understanding Paul's writings involves more than just trying to decipher run-on sentences, because in his letters we are dealing with a style of communication that is unlike our own. Issues and concerns of his time were addressed differently than they are in our times. And the way in which the people of his time made sense of the world around them influenced the very meaning of many of the words he used.

Let's begin by looking at four main ways in which Paul's style of communication differs from ours.

First, Paul's letters—indeed, all of the Septuagint translations of the Old Testament, all of the New Testament, and the writings of the early Church Fathers—were in Koine (pronounced: *coin-á*) Greek. So when we read these texts today, we are reading a modern-day English translation of what was written in an ancient language using an ancient style of dialogue.

Koine Greek had been the language of the common people in the Mediterranean area since a few hundred years before Paul's time. As a simplified form of the Greek language, Koine Greek had a more limited vocabulary than the more ancient Classical

Greek, and thus at times it can be difficult to translate it into modern languages.

For example, in Koine Greek, one would use the word *zymomenos* to express a strong feeling of annoyance.[1] The range of that feeling would then be discerned from the context in which the word was used. However, in English, the words angry, annoyed, vexed, irritated, exasperated, indignant, aggrieved, displeased, provoked, and resentful all convey variations of the strong feeling of annoyance.

Yet the word *zymomenos* also meant wrathful or rageful, which connotes a physical threat that is not conveyed by the English word "angry" or its synonyms. So to translate *zymomenos* into English as "angry," or as one of its synonyms, loses the physical threat aspect that might have been intended in the Koine Greek text.

In Paul's letters, we will encounter a number of words and phrases that had multiple meanings, or whose English "equivalent" in our translations lacks the full intent of the original Koine Greek words or phrases. Conversely, the English "equivalent" may express something different from what the original Koine Greek did.

Paul also confronted the problem that he had to convey some concepts for which there were no words or phrases in Koine Greek. For example, in trying to describe the divine nourishment, or sanctification, promised by Jesus, which today we call "grace," Paul used the Koine Greek word *charis*. But in the first century, there was no concept of God sanctifying human beings, so there was no word for it. Therefore, Paul had to use some word roughly close to this concept and hope that his listeners would get his point. The word *charis* actually meant "favor." And many even to this day think of grace as being a favor granted by God to those who live "virtuous"

---

[1]   William D. Mounce, *Basics of Biblical Greek* (Grand Rapids, MI: Zondervan, 2003).

lives, rather than being the divine nourishment we need to be able to do the will of God.

Second, in his letters, Paul was not teaching using story form, as did the writers of the Gospels. He was addressing issues and concerns of specific communities using the rhetorical style known as "diatribe." In Paul's day, a diatribe was a discourse that raised hypothetical questions and then responded to them. Or the speaker or writer stated false conclusions and then went on to refute them.

There was a great deal of subtlety to diatribe. Sometimes the refutation offered didn't actually answer the hypothetical question raised but instead spoke to the "real" issue the speaker or writer was addressing. In other cases, the listener needed to infer from the answer what the hypothetical question was. Therefore, modern listeners have a lot of difficulty when encountering the diatribe rhetorical form.

Additionally, the modern meaning of the word "diatribe" is very different than its ancient meaning. Today, a diatribe is a forceful and bitter verbal attack against someone or something. It is regarded as hostile, and so modern listeners may have the impression that Paul was often hostile toward those he was writing to.[2]

As an example of ancient diatribe what Paul wrote to the Corinthians: "Someone may say, 'How are the dead raised? With what kind of body will they come back?' You fool! What you sow is not brought to life unless it dies" (1 Cor. 15:35–36).

Here, Paul's adversary is hypothetically saying that the idea of the resurrection is foolish unless we understand what our new bodies will be like. Paul then responds to the question using the analogy of planting a seed. By speaking about the seed as a "body" that dies and comes to life, he points out that there is a change of attributes

---

[2]   Garry Wills, *What Paul Meant* (New York: Penguin Books, 2006).

in going from seed to plant. The old lifeform must be lost in order for the new lifeform to emerge. The new lifeform, the plant, is the ultimate destiny of the seed. Notice in this passage that Paul did not answer the hypothetical question about what kind of body we will come back with. Rather, he justified belief in the resurrection in a way that rendered meaningless the question of what kind of body we will have.

Third, in his letters, Paul often made use of a common rabbinic style of discourse known as "midrash."[3] Midrash was, and still is, the Jewish practice of interpreting a biblical passage in light of present conditions. In most cases, Paul relied on his Jewish listeners to know the passage(s) he was interpreting. Unfortunately, most of us do not know the passage(s), so we often misunderstand the point Paul was making.

As an example, in one of the most misunderstood passages in Paul's letters, he wrote:

> That no one is justified before God by the law is clear, for "the one who is righteous by faith will live." But the law does not depend on faith; rather, "the one who does these things will live by them." Christ ransomed us from the curse of the law by *becoming a curse for us*, for it is written, "Cursed be everyone who hangs on a tree." (Gal. 3:11–13)

At first, this passage can be very puzzling to us. It sounds like the "justified by faith alone" argument of the Reformation era. And Paul's remark about Christ being "cursed" is really baffling. But

---

[3]   Fr. Stanley B. Marrow, *Paul: His Letters and His Theology* (Mahwah, NJ: Paulist Press, 1986).

Paul was actually interpreting here three different passages from the Old Testament in making his point.

First, Paul was placing two verses of Scripture in juxtaposition: Habakkuk 2:4, "The just one who is righteous because of faith shall live," and Leviticus 18:5, "Keep, then, my statutes and decrees, for the person who carries them out will find life through them."

The underlying principle Paul was pointing out was that people do not become righteous (that is, have access to eternal life through being in right balance with God) by observing "the law" but, rather, through faith in God. Yet there is Law that must be observed. It is our means of accepting the gift of justification (having access to eternal life by being in right balance with God). Righteousness and justification cannot be earned; they must be actively and continually accepted. Note that Paul often used the terms righteousness and justification interchangeably, which differs from how other Scripture writers have used those terms.

Then Paul brought in Deuteronomy 21:22–23, which reads: "If a man guilty of a capital offense is put to death and you hang him on a tree, his corpse shall not remain on the tree overnight. You must bury it the same day; anyone who is hanged is a curse of God."[4]

Paul was making the point here that the "curse of the law" was that people were required to observe "the law," yet they could have no access to eternal life. The gates of Heaven were closed since the days of Adam and Eve. However, by Christ accepting the "curse" of being crucified, mankind was freed from the "curse" of having no access to eternal life in spite of diligently observing "the law."

You can see that if we didn't know the passages Paul was interpreting, our "understanding" of Galatians 3:11–13 might be "way off base."

---

[4]   To "hang on a tree" meant to crucify. The body of a crucified criminal was "cursed" in that it could defile the whole land if not immediately buried.

Fourth, every teaching reflects the theology of the teacher. What one is about to say or write must first "make sense" to the speaker or writer. So we need to know how Paul "made sense" of theological matters. That is, we need to have some understanding of his theology before we try to interpret his writings.[5]

The word "theology" technically means discourse about God. But it more broadly includes beliefs about other spiritual beings, such as angels or devils, and about human beings: whether we are inherently good or evil; why we behave the way we do; how we deal with sin; how we relate to God and our neighbor; and what happens to us when we die.

"Theology" also means the process through which we arrive at our theological beliefs. Whether we think of an individual believer who comes to faith or of an entire church that formulates its beliefs in a creedal statement, the process of clarifying one's beliefs may be thought of as "doing theology." And that process occupied much of Paul's life.

An important purpose of this short guide is to give you insights into Paul's theology. And in order to understand Paul's theology, we must understand first his "conversion," then an overview of his missionary life, and then the major themes that we can draw from his letters.

1.2 A Little Background

Paul was born a Jew in the predominantly Gentile (non-Jewish) city of Tarsus in the province of Cilicia (now southcentral Turkey). Since Tarsus was a Roman city, he was therefore a Roman citizen by birth, with both a Hebrew name (Saul) and a Greek name (Paul),

---

[5] Mary Ann Getty, *Paul and His Writings* (Oxford: Oxford University Press, 1990).

since Greek was the official public language of the Roman Empire at the time.[6]

Paul's Jewish pedigree was essential to his being believable to Jewish listeners, which is why Luke, in the Acts of the Apostles, wrote that Paul was brought up in Jerusalem (see Acts 22:3). This does not mean that he grew up in Jerusalem, only that he studied there under the rabbi Gamaliel, for a time. Paul grew up in the Gentile city of Tarsus, and just as his Jewish background was crucial to his fellow Jews, his deep knowledge of "Gentile ways" was important to his being an accepted teacher among Gentiles.

Gentiles were not godless people or irreligious; on the contrary, many were avid worshippers of gods—other than the one, true God—and they saw the Jewish insistence on only one God as blasphemy. Having many gods was seen by them as desirable, and each city had its favorite god. Even supreme leaders were regarded by Gentiles as gods, and Romans had patron gods for practically every aspect of life.[7]

The Romans prided themselves on religious tolerance. While they had "favorites," no god was considered better than another. Cults were also widespread in the Gentile world. Those cults specialized in secret rituals and "private mysteries." It was this religious tolerance that opened the door to people's willingness to listen to Paul's words. Most of Paul's initial resistance came from resentful Jews, not Gentiles, as while the Jews were very set in their religious practices, the Gentiles were eager to accept and adopt new religious communities with their own liturgies.

---

[6] Although Latin was spoken in Rome long before the birth of Christ, Latin was not the official language of the Roman Empire until the middle of the sixth century AD.

[7] This pagan concept of "patron gods" later gave rise to the concept of patron saints in the Christian era, which is why many today confuse the veneration of saints with the worship of saints.

Paul made three missionary journeys throughout the Eastern Mediterranean area that are recounted in the Acts of the Apostles:[8]

✠ First Missionary Journey (recounted in Acts 13:1–14:28)
✠ Second Missionary Journey (recounted in Acts 15:36–18:22)
✠ Third Missionary Journey (recounted in Acts 18:23–21:16)

His missionary journeys helped spread the gospel throughout much of the then-known world. Over the course of his ministry, Paul traveled more than 10,000 miles and established at least fourteen "churches" (or what we call today, dioceses).

The story of Paul in the Acts of the Apostles does not end with his martyrdom in Rome but with his arrival at Rome as a prisoner several years before his death. This fact has an important bearing on a number of the letters attributed to Paul.

1.3 OVERVIEW OF PAUL'S LETTERS

Most present-day biblical scholars divide the letters attributed to Paul into three categories, which are listed below. Whether or not a particular letter was written or dictated by Paul does not detract from the fact that all of the letters attributed to Paul are regarded as inspired by God:

✠ Primero-Pauline (those that appear to have been written by Paul): 1 Thessalonians, 1 Corinthians, 2 Corinthians, Galatians, Philippians, Philemon, and Romans

[8] Some scholars count as a Fourth Missionary Journey Paul's trip from Caesarea to Rome as a prisoner because he ministered to many people along the way (see Acts 21:27–28:31).

✠ Pastoral Letters (those that appear to have been written on Paul's behalf or at his request): Titus, 1 Timothy, and 2 Timothy

✠ Pseudo-Pauline (those that appear to have been written by Paul's disciples): Colossians, Ephesians, and 2 Thessalonians

In reading Scripture, we are mindful of who the author might be only to the extent that it helps us discern when it was written and, therefore:

✠ the point being made in the text and

✠ how it might have been understood by its first listeners, in their life circumstances.

This is a very important point, since there is no body of text that has undergone more scrutiny than have the letters attributed to Paul. Many religious leaders and groups have sought to shape the letters to fit their interpretation of the "good news" Paul proclaimed. As a result, the claim that "Paul didn't actually say that" has proliferated in many Bible studies in recent times, especially when modern translations of the Bible are read and studied according to today's understanding of certain words. In this book, we seek to hear Paul as the first-century missionary he was, not as a sixteenth-century theologian, as he has often been represented, especially in Protestant circles, or as a modern-day preacher.

Letter vs. Epistle

It's unlikely that Paul actually wrote much of his letters, although it is stated in Colossians 4:18, Galatians 6:11, and Philemon 19 that some of the text was in his own handwriting. In the ancient world, *charta* (papyrus sheets) were very expensive. So most letter writing was done for the letter author by a *grammateus* (scribe). Scholars have identified the likely scribe for a number of Paul's letters:

✣ Timothy (2 Corinthians, Philippians, and Philemon)
✣ Luke (Titus, 1 and 2 Timothy)
✣ Silvanus (1 Thessalonians)
✣ Sosthenes (1 Corinthians)
✣ Tertius (Romans)

The scribe wrote down the letter writer's dictation in shorthand, using a wooden stylus on a wax-covered wooden frame called a *diptych*. (Both Greek and Latin had shorthand forms in the first century.) To make a correction or change in the text, the scribe rubbed out the wax and rewrote it. That evening, the scribe would copy the text from the *diptych* to *charta* (parchment) using a *calamus*, or inked pen. He would then gently heat the *diptych* and smooth out the wax for the next use.

But whether each letter was written by Paul or by a scribe, we now need to address the difference between a "letter" and an "epistle," because failing to observe that distinction has led to much of the misinterpretation of Paul's writings. The distinction was first formally addressed by Gustav Adolf Deissmann, an early twentieth-century German theologian.[9] In the ancient world:

✣ an "epistle" was a literary work that usually presented a religious lesson or lessons and was intended for a general audience, whereas
✣ a "letter" was a nonliterary written communication from a writer to a specific person or group, which sometimes addressed some religious issue or issues.[10]

---

[9] Gustav Adolf Deissmann, *Light from the Ancient East* (London: Hodder and Stoughton, 1910).
[10] Jerome Murphy-O'Conner, *Paul the Letter-Writer: His World, His Opinions, His Skills* (Collegeville, MN: Liturgical Press, 1995).

The "epistles" in the New Testament are Hebrews, James, Jude, 1 John, and 1 and 2 Peter. All of the writings attributed to Paul are "letters," and of these, Ephesians has more the character of an encyclical than a personal letter.[11]

Paul wrote to encourage his converts, to praise their faith, and to counsel them on issues in their communities that had been brought to his attention; this counsel often included defending himself and defending what he had taught them. The letters purported to have been written on Paul's behalf, or by his disciples, sought to do the same. The culture of Paul's time was strongly structured around honor and shame. Honor was the esteem others held you in, and shame was the loss of honor through public challenge. Honor was the highest "virtue," transcending all others,[12] and so in virtually all of Paul's letters, he defended himself—his honor—against challengers. Although he eventually became a devoted follower of Jesus Christ, Paul did not entirely cease to view the world through the eyes of a Pharisee. This aspect appeared more clearly in some of Paul's letters than in others, reflecting the specific-occasion character of each of his letters.

In Paul's letters, there were some emotional overstatements, some eloquent exaggerations, some stern arguments, and even some pleading for his audience's understanding and support. Paul was not explicitly teaching theology and had no way of knowing the intense scrutiny his words would receive in future centuries. He was writing letters, not epistles. Today, calling them "epistles" sets the wrong expectations in the minds of modern readers and listeners.

---

[11] An "encyclical" was a type of letter that was intended to be read in one community after another, often following a circular path back to its starting point.

[12] Victor Matthews and Don Benjamin, *Social World of Ancient Israel* (Peabody, MA: Hendrickson Publishers, 1993).

Yet, collectively, Paul's letters put forth much of the foundation of what we know today as Christian theology. But this foundation was built a little in this passage, a little in that passage, and a little in another passage as he addressed specific issues in specific communities.

1.4 Paul's "Second Career"

As noted earlier, Luke's Acts of the Apostles ends with Paul arriving in Rome as a prisoner. This was about the year 61 AD. None of the details of Paul's travel or ministry recounted in what are known as Paul's Pastoral Letters fits the narrative in Acts. For example, in Acts, the only occasion Paul was in Crete was during the voyage that carried him as a prisoner to Rome. Yet the Letter to Titus indicates that Paul ministered in Crete for some time and left Titus there upon his departure. Indeed, there is no mention of Titus at all in Acts. Also, it is indicated in 1 Timothy that Paul installed Timothy as the first bishop of Ephesus, but there is no mention of this in Acts. Scripture was not intended to teach history, but the absence in the book of Acts of any of the details found in the Pastoral Letters can be puzzling.

Most scholars regard the details in the Pastoral Letters as fairly accurate. Therefore, these events had to have taken place after Paul first arrived in Rome in 61 AD; this hypothesis consequently posits the idea of a "second career." The theory is that Paul was released from prison in 63 AD, prior to the Great Fire of Rome in July 64 AD. Paul left Rome to minister in Crete, Ephesus, and Nicopolis, but then he was again arrested, probably in 66 AD, and brought back to Rome, where he was martyred in 67 AD.[13]

---

[13] Lindsey P. Pherigo, "Paul's Life after the Close of Acts," *Journal of Biblical Literature* 70, no. 4 (December 1951): 277ff.

1.5 THE SOCIAL ORDER IN PAUL'S WORLD

Paul lived in a culture that was very different from that of modern Western readers and listeners. He was a "second-Temple Jew," meaning that he grew up in the Pharisaic tradition, sharing and debating Scripture in the synagogues while the worship of God was centered in the Temple in Jerusalem. That Temple, which had been constructed after the Babylonian Exile period, was governed by the temple priests. Moreover, Paul saw the world as most other first-century Middle Easterners saw the world, as he lived in a community-centered culture in which "you are who others say you are."

Because Paul did not live in modern times in a Western culture, we need to understand his letters in the cultural context in which they were written. Scholars have spent a great deal of effort to identify who wrote each letter, when, and to whom, so that we might take into account the worldview and life circumstances of the letter's first listeners.

One of the difficulties we face today is that Western listeners have been saturated with descriptions of Paul and interpretations of his words and actions that date from the Reformation period (1517–1563). But Paul was not from the Reformation period. He was from the first century; and we need some preliminary understanding of how Paul and others of the first century interpreted the world around them.

We can understand Paul and his world by studying his culture's "symbolic universe," or cultural worldview. A symbolic universe is the set of cultural norms and beliefs that "everyone in the group knows" and by which the group makes sense of the world around them and institutionalizes what they regard as acceptable behavior.[14]

---

[14] Peter Berger and Thomas Luckmann, *The Social Construction of Reality* (New York: Anchor Books, 1966).

Many anthropologists have concluded that symbolic universes can be characterized along these six dimensions:[15]

✶ Order: patterns and their explanations
✶ Body: perceptions of the human body
✶ Cosmology: what is in the world and why
✶ Misfortune and Suffering: explanations for why they exist
✶ Sin: what is it and what are its origins
✶ Rituals: the rites that confirm values and institutions and reestablish order.

Utilizing those six dimensions, biblical anthropologists describe the symbolic universe in which Paul grew up, and which he shared with most of those he encountered in his missionary life, in the following framework:

Order: Paul and his contemporaries perceived that everything in the world had its proper place. They feared anarchy and chaos. Order, and the maintaining of order, was of central importance in their lives. So they were naturally authoritarian and hierarchical. Each person had their "proper place": male/female, child/adult, slave/freeman, Jew/Gentile, etc.

This order reflected the nature of God. Jewish Scripture, which stated that "I, the Lord your God, am holy" (Lev. 19:2), was taken to mean that God was the ultimate of orderliness. God expressed his holiness by creating an orderly universe with a proper structure of relationships. And the central means of establishing order was to separate things and people that did not belong together.

A careful reading of the Creation Story in Genesis shows that it's actually a story about God separating things that did not belong together. For example: "God saw that the light was good. God then

---

[15] Mary T. Douglas, *Natural Symbols* (London: Routledge Classics, 1996).

separated the light from the darkness" (Gen. 1:4). And "God made the dome, and it *separated* the water below the dome from the water above the dome" (Gen. 1:7). And "the water under the sky was gathered into its basin, and the dry land appeared" (Gen. 1:9). Again, "God said: Let there be lights in the dome of the sky, to *separate* day from night" (Gen. 1:14). And so on. The ancient Jewish people saw God's primary act of creating as bringing order out of chaos: order through which mankind might prosper.

This is a really important concept for us to understand. In our times, we interpret Creation as an expression of God's love, and we acknowledge His desire to share that love with His creatures. But first-century Middle Easterners interpreted Creation as the ultimate expression of God's orderliness. To them, mankind knew of God's holiness by observing the order of nature: God wisely separated things and put them in their "proper" places. God then gave man dominion over His ordered creation (see Gen. 1:26, 28) — to keep things orderly.[16]

Even the Temple in Jerusalem reflected the "proper ordering" of things. There was a designated area for Gentiles, a designated area for women, a designated area for men, a designated area for priests, and a designated area for the High Priest. If one entered the wrong designated area, the penalty was death.

Time was also ordered: the Jews had special hours of prayer, special holidays, and specific offerings for specific times and events. Their rites of purification sought to put things back in their "right place," to restore order. Things, persons, or conduct that was in the "wrong place" were seen as polluting and threatening to the whole social group.

[16] Jerome H. Neyrey, *Paul, In Other Words: A Cultural Reading of His Letters* (Louisville, KY: John Knox Press, 1990).

In the end, good fences made good neighbors; order made it clear where "you and your things belong" and where "I and my things belong." Trespassing was treated as a grave social breach. Boundaries were to be strictly observed, not out of selfishness but out of respect for order. To them, to be disorderly was to be unholy.

Body: Control over the physical body both encouraged and reflected social order. The more bodily behaviors were controlled, the more orderly society would be. Therefore, all bodily disorder, including illness and injury, was regarded as resulting from a failure to control one's body.

For human beings, all bodily controls are learned; they arise out of cultural norms. What is proper and what is not proper has to be instilled from an early age and regularly reinforced. Just as a community's boundaries could be threatened, so a body's boundaries could be threatened. So there was great concern over what entered and left the body. An "unholy" body, i.e., one that was not under control, could not come into the presence of God (see Lev. 21:16–20). Special rituals were required to remove such "unholiness."

In the cultural worldview of the ancient Jews, a drunk man had failed to control his bodily behavior; this failure made him a danger to the community, because he could not adequately protect those in his charge or come to other's aid in a time of emergency.

Additionally, if any one person came into contact with another person's bodily fluids, he or she was made "unholy," because the fluids were not in their "proper place." Yet the observation of one rule often led to the violation of another rule. For example, married couples were to have frequent intercourse so that they could have many children: "God said to them: Be fertile and multiply" (Gen. 1:28a). Nevertheless, to follow this command made the husband "unholy," because his fluid was out of its "proper place." This required him to engage in a "purifying" ritual bath and to have no contact with his wife or the synagogue until the next sundown.

Moreover, a body that was not complete or that was deformed in some way was not "holy," because it did not exhibit proper order. Since what entered or left the body could make one "unholy," even saying something or hearing something or touching something (or someone) at the "wrong time or place" made one "unholy."

The ancient Jews also understood that a body had hierarchical order, the head being the most important and the feet being the least. What entered through the sense of sight was more important than what entered through the sense of touch, and so on. By Paul's referring to the Church as a "body," he was assigning the same control expectations over that "body's" behavior and the same sense of hierarchy as his audience would have applied to a physical body.

To first century people, an apostle (one sent by Christ) was more important than an elder (one who presided over the Breaking of the Bread), who was more important than a preacher (one who proclaimed the word), and so on.

This principle had great importance to Paul, for his opponents insisted that he was a preacher; whereas Paul insisted that he was an apostle. To Paul, the wholeness of the Body of Christ was threatened by any division or discord (interpreted as disorder) among its members.

Cosmology: In the worldview of Paul and his contemporaries, nothing happened by coincidence; everything that happened was caused by God. They envisioned a cosmic duel going on between Good and Evil. In the ancient world, when Genesis referred to "the tree of knowledge of good and evil" (Gen. 2:17), it was referring to Good and Evil as personified beings, one an agent of God, the other an enemy of God; both had influence over mankind. And so, to the ancient Jews, Adam and Eve having knowledge of Good and

Evil made them part of the cosmic struggle between Good and Evil, a struggle which God sought to keep them from.

For centuries, Jews saw Satan not as the embodiment of Evil but as the false accuser of the people before God—an enemy of the people rather than an enemy of God. The Book of Job is an excellent example of the ancient Jewish understanding of Satan.

The Jews also thought it was fruitless for humans to try to figure out why there was Evil—there just was! They envisioned a whole army of enemies of God at work in the world: death, rulers, tempters, demons, Rome, evil spirits, and the power of darkness, just to name a few. Even Sin was seen as a personified force opposing God.

Yet despite their portrayal of God as the creative orderer of the cosmos, God was also perceived as acting in ways that upset traditional patterns of order. What should be orderly was sometimes changed, for reasons that were not always apparent. For example, although God created mankind in His image and likeness, the world was divided into dualistic camps of good and bad people, good and bad foods, good and bad animals, good and bad weather, and so on. God's promise to Abraham was seen in dualistic terms against the law given to Moses: blessings vs. curses; spirit vs. flesh; freedom vs. slavery; inheritance vs. dispossession; worthiness vs. unworthiness; believers vs. unbelievers.

Paul's audience did not understand night as the absence of daylight; it was a sinister entity unto itself. They did not travel at night, not primarily for lack of light, but because night was the realm of the malevolent. That's why God separated night from daytime. And death was not the absence of life but a sinister entity that reigned over the earth, because everyone was subject to death. Paul spoke of death as "the last enemy" of Christ (1 Cor. 15:26).

Misfortune and Suffering: To Paul and his contemporaries, the world was a very unjust place because Evil was always attacking

Good. Misfortune was the working of malevolent forces, agents of Evil. And misfortune could only be dealt with through appeasing those evil forces in the world. Often, one's immediate response to misfortune was "who did this to me?" (Today, the reaction is "why me?") Even a storm at sea was interpreted as the working of evil spirits. Dying was a misfortune caused by the power of death working through malevolent forces.

Spirits were seen to have great power over one's life. While there were some good spirits in the world, illness in particular was often viewed as being possessed by evil spirits. Evil spirits could cause the misfortune of being led astray and making blasphemous statements about God. Misfortune was sometimes seen as a form of "unjust" suffering.

Suffering was seen as punishment for being disorderly ("unholy") or for being out of "proper order." One's response to suffering was "what did I do to deserve this?" In some cases, suffering was seen as a result of domestic hostility. Suffering could only be alleviated by restoring order, so much of the work of ancient "physicians" was to engage in rituals that sought to restore order in the one who was suffering. In the process of healing, these early "physicians" used some primitive medicinals and salves, which gave them some credibility as healers.

Sin: Those who were "ungodly" were seen as being under the power of Sin (here the personified being known as Sin). So when Paul wrote that Christians were "freed from [the slavery of] sin" (Rom. 6:17–18), this did not mean that they were no longer prone to sinful behavior but that, through Christ, they were freed from the power of the personified being Sin.

The personification of Sin evolved over a very long period. In the years leading up to and during the early stages of the Babylonian Captivity, the people saw themselves as victims of God's wrath because of the bad things their kings and priests did. Throughout much of Jewish history, to be sinful was to be out of "proper order" because someone broke a rule; Sin had exercised power over them.

But in the Adam and Eve story in Genesis, which first appeared around the year 560 BC, those in the Babylonian Captivity learned that sin arose from the disposition of their hearts and that sin was breaking their relationship with God. They now understood that each person had a personal responsibility for sin. This is a very important point for us to understand. In the absence of a person accepting personal responsibility for his or her sin, the salvific act of Jesus Christ would have little personal significance to the sinner.

Sadly, over the years following the Babylonian Captivity, around 457 BC and later, so many rules and "commandments" were added to Mosaic Law that had to be carefully observed that one frequently had to break one rule in order to keep another. And so the Jewish people were frequently in the state of being "sinful" out of shear circumstances. The personification of Sin gave them an "acceptable" reason for their "sinful" condition: "Sin made me do it."[17]

When Paul wrote to the Romans that he was subject to two laws, the law of God and the law of Sin (see Rom. 7:22–23), he was referring to the personified being Sin, an enemy of God whose power over human beings rivaled God's power. And the "law of God" was the Ten Commandments, not the Mosaic Law.

Rituals: First-century peoples believed that they needed fastidiously performed rites in order to expel the ill that had permeated their lives and to restore and maintain proper order. A ritual marked a transition from one's present state to a more ordered state. Each ritual had to have the appropriate presider: husband, father, male elder, physician, rabbi, Temple priest, High Priest.

---

[17] The mantra "the devil made me do it" emerged during the Christian era.

For example, a wedding feast was a social ritual presided over by the father of the groom that marked the transition of the bride and groom's families from being separate families to being one family—a new order was established in the community. So at a wedding feast, it was the families that were being married. The couple was already married at the betrothal ritual, which was presided over by the father of the bride.

A presentation of a firstborn son in the Temple was a social ritual presided over by the child's mother. It involved a sacrifice that marked the child's dedication to the Lord and the mother's purification from her "unclean" state. The birth had placed her body in a "disordered" state, as bleeding and other maladies had prevented her from functioning as a wife. Through the presentation rite, proper order was restored to the family's lives.

A circumcision was a social ritual presided over by a rabbi, and it marked a male's transition from being among the unchosen to being among the chosen. A new order was established for that person.

A fence-mending was a social ritual presided over by a rabbi that restored proper order in the community after a trespassing or boundary transgression. Both the offender and the offended needed to be "cleansed" of their disordered states.

A divorce was a social ritual presided over by a rabbi that marked the transition in the couple's life from a disordered state to an ordered state—what did not belong together was separated.

An excommunication, or "unbinding," was a social ritual presided over by a rabbi that marked one's transition from being among the community of faithful to being an outsider. One who did not belong was separated from the community, thus restoring proper order.

A funeral was a social ritual presided over by the eldest able-bodied person in the family, and it marked one's transition from this world to Sheol (or the underworld). Again, a new order was established for that person.

A *he'tot* was a social ritual presided over by a Temple priest. It involved an animal sacrifice and marked a person's transition from being defiled or "unclean" to being "clean," restoring the person to proper order in their life and the community.

The Day of Atonement was a social ritual each year presided over by the High Priest, and it involved a special sacrifice that made reparations for the sins of the people, "cleansing" them of their sins and reestablishing proper order among the people of God.

And so we see, as was stated at the outset, that the people of Paul's world feared anarchy and chaos. Maintaining proper order was central to their sustained existence and their seeking godliness. Their lives were steeped in rituals that sought to restore and maintain life in its proper order.

1.6 PAUL'S CONVERSION

When used in a religious context, the word "conversion" involves much more than a change in one's attitudes or outlook. It involves a break with what was and an embracing of what one has become.

To Luke, Paul's experience on the road to Damascus was a vocational call, not a conversion. Paul's conversion took place over time as a result of the Damascus event. Luke gives three accounts of the event in Acts 9:3–8, 22:6–11, and 26:13–19. He saw Paul's conversion not as a rupture of Paul's faith in Judaism but as an evolving acknowledgment of Jesus as the Messiah, the fulfillment of Judaism. Luke treated the event at Damascus akin to a theophany (a revelation of God) similar to what Abraham, Jacob, Moses, and Samuel experienced, as while Paul was aware of God (Jesus) speaking to him, we have no indication that Paul actually saw Jesus—unlike the Apostles, who had seen the Risen Jesus.

In contrast, Paul's account of the Damascus event in Galatians 1:11–24 sounds like an "instant conversion." Here, Paul was defending a charge against him in Galatia that he was not a legitimate "apostle" (that is, one sent by Christ). Paul saw his calling as having come from before his birth, just as Jeremiah did (see Gal. 1:15–16; cf. Jer. 1:5), and the event at Damascus was his awakening and the origin of his apostleship (see 1 Cor. 15:8; 1 Cor. 9:1). To Paul, he did not "convert" from one religion (Judaism) to another (Christianity); rather, he matured in his understanding of God and His plan for all mankind.

While Luke and his listeners saw coming to Christ as breaking with one religion (paganism) and moving to another (Christianity), Paul saw his "conversion" not as a matter of coming upon the "pearl of great price," as Luke's listeners did, but as responding to an invitation to move from worthless efforts to efforts that fulfilled the will of God (see Phil. 3:7–8). For Paul to regard his hard-earned righteousness, "based on the law," as worthless must have been a difficult struggle, especially since he had initially seen Christianity as a grave threat to his Judaism and his understanding of himself and had viewed his pre-conversion efforts to destroy Christianity as a personal crusade.

And so Paul's conversion was a reversal of the ordering of his values, making his vision of all things utterly new. He was "called for a mission." Paul did not try to describe his conversion, because his encounter with Jesus had completely altered his entire earthly existence. Indeed, he was not "converted"; he was "made new."

Paul saw conversion as a gift of the Holy Spirit, not something someone does. Luke saw Paul's conversion as a mighty work of the Holy Spirit. (Indeed, the title "Acts of the Apostles," first used by Irenaeus in the late second century, would more appropriately be: "The Mighty Works of the Holy Spirit.") But, today, many continue to see conversion as something someone chooses to do. So, in recent centuries, we have become accustomed to thinking of Paul as he was portrayed by Luke in Acts, rather than as he described himself in his letters.

1.7 THE "THREAT" OF CHRISTIANITY

As Christians, we are not accustomed to thinking of Christianity as "threatening." However, to those who are not Christians, Christianity can be perceived as very threatening, because it brings with it a symbolic universe, or social worldview, that is substantially at odds with the prevailing non-Christian worldview. And this was most definitely the case in Paul's time. Much of his opposition came from those who were disturbed by the Christian worldview he presented, as it upset their well-established "proper order" of things and the dictates and management of that order.

For example, in Christianity, God had a new set of "chosen people," and Christian communities were to be inclusive of those who were not "like us." Christ had brought forth a new perception of order. The established social hierarchy was greatly disturbed—none were "set apart." Social positions were turned upside down—the poor were the favored ones of God, not those who were well off. Even within the new Christian communities, the mingling of Jewish Christians and Gentile Christians was very problematic; who was circumcised and who was not was a very big deal, and "they are not like us" meant for many that there was disorder in the community.

The changes in worldview seemed endless to the ancient Jews. The Crucifixion of Christ exhibited "the power of God and the wisdom of God" at work (1 Cor. 1:24), not the humiliation of a condemned one; this understanding negated their concept of honor ("you are who others say you are"). Christians understood Creation as an expression of God's love, not His orderliness; instead, the Final Judgment will be the time of ultimate orderliness. Furthermore, Christians understood that God was free to be gracious to any one

He pleased; but many others viewed this belief as God being unjust (see Rom. 9:14). And if these shifts in worldview weren't enough, on a more practical level, even God's "day of rest" was changed to the First Day of the week.

Paul himself struggled with the Christian worldview that upset the one he grew up with and had invested so much of his life in. For example, he advocated no fellowship between believers and non-believers, because the presence of non-believers brought disorder into the lives of believers. In his thinking, even the triune nature of God had to reflect proper ordering, which, in the ancient worldview, was the essence of holiness.

Shifting from one worldview to another is a very difficult process. We will see in his letters that Paul was working from both worldviews in the same letter and sometimes in the very same passage. Therefore, in some cases, he presented Christian concepts using terminologies from the ancient worldview.

In considering just how threatening the Christian worldview was in Paul's time, it's easy to see why the Roman authorities labeled Christianity as a "dangerous superstition." It challenged the long-held "proper order" of things and proclaimed that a crucified rabbi from the outback (the name Galilee means "the outback") was actually a divine being, while Caesar was not. In time, this "threat" led to the martyrdom of Peter and Paul in Rome and of thousands of other Christians throughout the Roman Empire.

1.8 PREPARING TO ENTER PAUL'S LETTERS

There is a very important matter we need to address before we enter into Paul's letters. Paul's letters—indeed, the whole of the Bible—are not just ancient writings but the inspired word of God. They are Sacred Scripture. This means that we must come to Paul's letters with a very different mindset than we would for any other text.

Sacred Scripture, and the workings of the Holy Spirit, is the avenue that God chose to reveal Himself and His plan of salvation for all mankind, and He therefore makes Himself known through texts produced by inspired writers, including St. Paul. God's message to His people is timeless, but it is embedded in the words, imagery, and forms of communication that are rooted in the times in which each text was written.

In reading Sacred Scripture, we are faced with a two-stage discernment process. First, we need to assess what the text likely meant at the time it was written and what the author's intended missive was for the first listeners. Second, with that understanding, we then seek to discern what divine, timeless message was intended for God's people, including us.

As we progress through Paul's letters, we will need to keep in mind that approaching his letters with an anthropological perspective might make Paul appear less relevant, even problematic, to our times, as we will be made more keenly aware that he, and his first listeners, shared a worldview and manner of communicating that are very different from ours. When we take his worldview into account, however, we can better understand the message that was intended in Sacred Scripture.

As was stated earlier, much of the interpretations of Paul's words found in modern-day literature comes from the debates during the period of the Protestant Reformation. And for much of history, Paul's letters were interpreted in the context of the times in which the texts were read, not the times in which they were written. Unfortunately, this method of interpretation has led to confusion, and sometimes heated arguments and frustration, for those who sought only clarity. In this book, we will come to Paul's letters from the perspective of his first listeners. We seek to hear them "anew" and draw from them insights we may not have heard or considered before.

We cannot ignore the fact that there are a number of phrases, passages, and whole letters that have been debated by scholars for good reason, and these debates are often inconclusive. So when we come to those areas of disagreement, we will consider the different viewpoints and bring to bear the theological perspective given us in the *Catechism of the Catholic Church*:

1. There is a unity to the whole of Scripture. All are part of God's mysterious and unfolding revelation of Himself and His plan of salvation (see *CCC* 112).
2. Recognizing the role of the Holy Spirit in guiding the process of interpretation throughout history, interpretations need to be consistent with "the living Tradition of the whole Church" (see *CCC* 113).
3. There is a mutual consistency to the whole of Scripture. Though we may not comprehend every detail of God's plan of salvation, there is a "coherence of truths" embedded in Scripture (see *CCC* 114).

Therefore, in order to properly assess Paul's letters and how they are interpreted, we will seek the guidance of the Holy Spirit as we view Paul and his writings in the larger context of Old and New Testament passages and events. For God's revelation does not contradict itself. And as we keep in mind the theological perspective given us in the *Catechism of the Catholic Church*—the unity in Scripture, the role of the Holy Spirit, and the mutual consistency of Scripture—we can be assured that if our conclusion about the divine message embedded in a particular text is contrary to what is known of God and His plan from elsewhere in Scripture, then our conclusion is incorrect, and it needs further study and discernment.

This mutual consistency in Sacred Scripture applies to God's revelation of Himself and His plan for salvation. It does not mean that every detail or even descriptions of the same event or situation will be consistent. Indeed, in Middle Eastern writings, we find quite the opposite, as we saw earlier in the two quite different descriptions of Paul's conversion.

Ancient Middle Eastern communication was always a partnership exchange: the speaker or writer was responsible for conveying the lesson, and it was the responsibility of the listeners to discern the lesson. The "message" in ancient Middle Eastern communications was not conveyed primarily in the plot but in the details used in the communication. Details of an event or situation were omitted if they did not relate to the intended lesson; or the details could even be altered somewhat to support the lesson.[18]

We saw earlier, in section 1.6, that Paul used his description of his conversion in addressing a very different situation than did Luke. Therefore, the details each chose to use in relating the story were quite different. This is not an inconsistency in the Bible, it is a characteristic of ancient Middle Eastern writing.

After we acknowledge this difference in accounts, we can move to the second stage of our discernment: what is the timeless message intended for us? Let us continue to look at Luke's and Paul's differing accounts of Paul's conversion. We need to recognize first that Sacred Scripture has been quite consistent on conversion and its necessity: in the lives of the patriarchs, in the lives of the prophets, in the lives of all human beings. Indeed, Jesus said: "Unless you turn [convert] and become like children, you will not enter the kingdom of heaven" (Matt. 18:3). All of us must break with what was and embrace our being children of God. Notice that Jesus was not referring to our entering Heaven, but rather the *Kingdom of Heaven*. As we will see

[18] Robert Alter, *The Art of Biblical Narrative* (New York: Basic Books, 2011).

later in section 3.6, the Kingdom of Heaven is a way of living in which Christ reigns in the hearts of believers as they strive to fulfill the will of God in this life. God cannot reign in our hearts unless we are like children, open to His love and guidance. Conversion is therefore an ongoing process in our lives (although some may experience a sudden awakening that they perceive as being their "conversion"). As we embrace the timeless message about conversion, we realize that whether Paul's conversion was as related in Acts or as in Galatians really doesn't matter. Sacred Scripture teaches faith lessons, not history lessons.

It is in carefully following the two-stage discernment process that we will come to gain what was meant for us through Paul's letters. So, asking the Holy Spirit to accompany us, we enter into Paul's letters in what many scholars regard as the approximate order in which they were written.

TWO

✠ ✠ ✠

THE FIRST LETTER TO
THE THESSALONIANS

2.1 SOME BACKGROUND

In about 50 AD, Paul arrived in Greece for the first time. Soon afterwards, Timothy joined him there. In making converts in Philippi and, soon afterwards, in Thessalonica, Paul was beset by intense opposition, principally from resentful Jews. Moving on to Beroea, he was again harassed by enemies from Thessalonica, and he hurriedly left for Athens. Silas and Timothy remained behind for a while in Beroea. Paul soon sent Timothy back to Thessalonica to strengthen that community in its trials.

Timothy and Silas finally returned to Paul when he reached Corinth, probably in the early summer of 51 AD. Timothy returned with a report on conditions at Thessalonica, which served as the occasion for Paul writing this letter, the shortest of his surviving letters.

The principal divisions of this letter are:

✠ Address (1:1–10)
✠ Previous Relations with the Thessalonians (2:1–3:13)
✠ Specific Exhortations (4:1–5:25)
✠ Final Greeting (5:26–28)

2.2 THE CALL TO EVANGELIZE

Thessalonica was a large city located on the crossroads of a great Roman trade route, the Via Egnatia. It featured a deep seaport on the Aegean Sea on the delta of the Axios River, and it was the ideal location to find new potential listeners to the Christian message.

In Judaism, anyone who evangelized but was not specifically trained as a rabbi was shunned and sometimes forcefully expelled from the community, just as Paul had been expelled from Thessalonica. This practice reflected what the Jews referred to as "the traditions of our ancestors" (see Mark 7:5; Matt. 15:2; John 7:22): unwritten laws governing proper conduct.

Paul, however, was keenly aware that all Christians were called to the mission of evangelization, not just those who were sent (the "apostles"). He was convicted in his belief that each Christian's election to the mission of evangelization was made by God and proceeded from His love (see 1 Thess. 1:4). It was not special training but the action of the Holy Spirit that rendered one's words persuasive (see 1 Thess. 1:5). The core of the message of evangelization was the gospel ("good news") of salvation, which was foretold by the prophets and was brought to fulfillment by Jesus Christ.

So Paul began this letter by trying to infuse in his listeners the desire to evangelize, because the very proclamation of the "good news" told those willing to listen that they were beloved by God. The Thessalonians had turned to God (see 1 Thess. 1:9), and this turn was exemplified by their proclaiming the "good news." God reads each heart (see 1 Thess. 2:4), and therefore each Christian must pass on the Word of God faithfully (see 1 Thess. 2:13). The very best form of evangelizing is by example (see 1 Thess. 2:11–12), and so Paul told the Thessalonians that Christians do not work for earthly reward but instead must be motivated by love of God and love of others (see 1 Thess. 2:7–9).

Of course, this call to every Christian to evangelize persists to this day, and, as Paul advised his listeners, all Christians must rely on prayer to make their work fruitful (see 1 Thess. 3:10).

2.3 THE IMMINENT *PAROUSIA*

In this letter, Paul defended his manner of teaching, but more importantly, he pointed out that the proclamation of the gospel was first and foremost the work of the Holy Spirit.[19] The Holy Spirit works through human beings who, to the best of their ability, communicate the gospel's power with full conviction (see 1 Thess. 1:5). But a proclamation of the word is in vain if the listeners do not embrace it. So Paul insisted that the gospel is "good news" only to one who has faith.

It is evident from Paul's letter that Jewish itinerate preachers, identifying themselves as Christians, had come to Thessalonica claiming that there would be no *Parousia* (Second Coming of Christ), which was contrary to what Paul had taught. The Thessalonians were very troubled by this, and they were seeing people dying without experiencing the promised *Parousia*. They were asking: "Since Jesus hasn't returned yet, what happens to those believers who died?"

In the mid-first century, people were expecting Jesus' return "any day now." This is referred to as the expectation of an Imminent *Parousia*. Paul was convinced of the Imminent *Parousia*, and his teachings reflected that expectation. Paul noted that what God had promised had already become a reality in Jesus. Therefore, the Thessalonians could accept the proclamation of the gospel as the word of God because it was already at work in them (see 1 Thess. 2:13). "If we believe that Jesus died and rose, so too will God, through Jesus, bring with him those who have fallen asleep" (1 Thess. 4:14).

---

[19] Margaret Fromer and Shar Keyes, *Letters to the Thessalonians* (Wheaton, IL: Harold Shaw Publishers, 1975).

Notice that in his response, Paul avoided being drawn into the argument over "when is Jesus coming?" He only stated that Jesus *was* coming back. Furthermore, he said, "we shall always be with the Lord" (1 Thess. 4:17), whether we witness the *Parousia* or not. This is an example of ancient diatribe. This method of reshaping a question into one that could be answered appears in a number of Paul's responses.

2.4 "DID PAUL ACTUALLY SAY THAT?"

We have already noted that one often hears in present-day Bible studies something along the lines of: "Paul didn't actually say that!" This is often the case when one encounters the following passage, which appears to blame the Jewish people for killing not only Jesus Christ but also the prophets:

> For you, brothers, have become imitators of the churches of God that are in Judea in Christ Jesus. For you suffer the same things from your compatriots as they did from the Jews, *who killed both the Lord Jesus and the prophets* and persecuted us; they do not please God, and are opposed to everyone, trying to prevent us from speaking to the Gentiles that they may be saved, thus constantly filling up the measure of their sins. But the wrath of God has finally begun to come upon them. (1 Thess. 2:14–16)

This is often pointed to as the "proof text" that Paul, and therefore the Bible, "taught" anti-Semitism.[20] For many years, biblical scholars

---

[20] Wills, *What Paul Meant.*

argued that this text must have been a later addition to Paul's letter, because it was inconsistent with things Paul had to say about Jews elsewhere,[21] such as: "my brothers, my kin according to the flesh; they are Israelites; theirs the adoption, the glory, the covenants, the giving of the law, the worship, and the promises; theirs the patriarchs, and from them, according to the flesh, is the Messiah" (Rom. 9:3b–5a).

For a long while, the claim that the passage in 1 Thessalonians was a later addition appeared plausible, since the first evidence of anti-Semitism among Christians was when Christianity became the official state religion of the Roman Empire in 380 AD. Yet this text was in the oldest surviving manuscript of Paul's letter, the *Codex Vaticanus*, which dates from the early 300s AD.[22]

However, more recently, as we have become increasingly familiar with the times in which Paul lived, many have come to see that the term "the Jews" in this 1 Thessalonians passage has been misinterpreted because it is being heard and understood in the context of the current meaning of those words.

The word that is translated into modern English Bibles as "the Jews" is the Greek word *ioudaioi*. The Greek translation of Jewish scripture, the Septuagint, which was produced before the birth of Christ, does indeed translate the ancient Hebrew word for God's Chosen People, *yehudim* ("the descendants of Judah"), as *ioudaioi*. But by the first century AD, the Hebrew people referred to themselves not as *ioudaioi* but as *israēlitēi* ("Israelites"). And *israēlitēi* is the term Paul used in the above passage from Romans 9. The term *ioudaioi* ("the Jews"), however, was at this time used for the Jewish authorities, both civil and religious. A similar shift in meaning is seen in the

---

[21] Fr. Raymond E. Brown, *The Death of the Messiah*, vol. 2 (New Haven, CT: Yale University Press, 1994).

[22] "Codex Vaticanus," in *Catholic Encyclopedia* (Nashville, TN: Thomas Nelson Inc., 1990).

Greek word *hellenes*, which is usually translated as "Greeks" but really refers to Gentiles in general, not just specifically the Greek people.

In the Old Testament, it was the Jewish authorities, not the Jewish people, who killed the prophets. And the people of Paul's time certainly knew that it was the Jewish authorities, not the people, who forced Pilate to condemn Christ to crucifixion. So the text does not appear to be a later insertion after all but a devastating misinterpretation of what Paul said. As Frederick Danker, the preeminent Koine Greek lexicographer of the twentieth century, put it:

> Incalculable harm has been caused by simply glossing *Ioudaioi* with "Jew"; for many readers and auditors of Bible translations do not practice the historical judgment necessary to distinguish between circumstances and events of an ancient time and contemporary ethnic-religious-social realities, with the result that anti-Semitism in the modern sense of the term is needlessly fostered through faulty biblical text interpretations.[23]

So, following the principle that there is a mutual consistency to the whole of Scripture (see *CCC* 114), "the Jews" cannot at the same time be both God's Chosen People in the Old Testament and the "despised people" in the New Testament. An anti-Semitism interpretation of 1 Thessalonians 2:14–16 has to be incorrect.[24]

---

[23] Frederick William Danker, "Ioudaios," in *A Greek-English Lexicon of the New Testament and Other Early Christian Literature* (Chicago: University of Chicago Press, 2009).

[24] We encounter a similar misinterpretation of the term "the Jews" in the Gospel of John, which has likewise prompted many to claim that the New Testament is anti-Semitic.

2.5 SOME OTHER INSIGHTS

As we "listen" to Paul's letters, we need to remember that in many respects, we are eavesdropping on a different culture. This is particularly true in 1 Thessalonians, in which we encounter words and phrases whose meaning we have come to take for granted. Yet these words and phrases had a different connotation to Paul's first listeners.

In his opening, Paul praised the Christians in Thessalonica, saying that, "you turned to God from idols to serve the living and true God" (1 Thess. 1:9). Further, Paul exhorted them to "conduct yourselves as worthy of the God who calls you into his kingdom" (1 Thess. 2:12). We usually take these passages to mean that the people had moved from being pagans to being Christians, but that's not the way those in the first century would have interpreted them. Paul was referring here to "the living and true God" — the singular, only God. This means that, in their worldview of the cosmic struggle between Good and Evil, if there is only one God, then those in His Kingdom must be on the side of Good, and all who are not in His Kingdom must be on the side of Evil. In their worldview, there was no middle ground; there was no coexistence among those who sided with Good and those who sided with Evil. This presented serious social challenges for early Christians, as just about every aspect of an ancient person's interactions with others involved some form of homage or sacrifice to gods. Even sharing a meal with others was a "sacred" experience. To what extent could Christians continue to associate with those who were "on the side of Evil" without bringing disorder into their own lives?

As another example, in 1 Thessalonians 4:3–8, Paul referred to "impurity." We usually take this word as having a sexual or immoral connotation. But, in the worldview of Paul's first audience, something was "impure" if it was disordered in some way. In the case of this passage, the disorder was marriages between siblings and close blood relatives. These were common among Gentiles but were regarded by Jews (and Christians) as "disordered" and, therefore, "impure."

In yet another example, Paul said to the Thessalonians, "Do not quench the Spirit" (1 Thess. 5:19). We usually take this to mean that we should be open to the promptings of the Holy Spirit. But recall that the ancient Jews and first Christians understood that order in their daily lives was reflected by orderliness in their bodily actions. "Responding to the Spirit" often meant charismatic behavior and speaking in tongues. But to Paul's first audience, this behavior was evidence of a failure to control one's bodily actions: it therefore signified acting disorderly. So the exhortation to "not quench the Spirit" had to later be refined by Paul and others (see 1 Cor. 14:1–40; 2 Thess. 2:1–15).

It was noted earlier, in section 1.1, that we don't usually find theological statements in Paul's letters in neat, cogent form. Rather, we find some of it here and some of it there throughout his letters. The staff of the Navarre Bible, in their commentary on 1 Thessalonians, point out a very good example of that.[25] Written only about twenty years after Christ's death and Resurrection, this letter contains, here and there, the main elements of the Christian faith that we know now as the Apostles Creed. In this letter, Paul taught that God is our Father (see 1 Thess. 1:3); Jesus is His Son (see 1 Thess. 1:9–10); salvation is brought about "through our Lord Jesus Christ who died for us" (1 Thess. 5:9–10) and "rose" (1 Thess. 4:14). He will come again (see 1 Thess. 2:19, 3:13) in power and majesty (see 1 Thess. 4:16) to judge (see 1 Thess. 4:6) the living and the dead

---

[25] *The Navarre Bible: Thessalonians and Pastoral Letters* (Dublin: Four Courts Press, 1992).

(1 Thess. 4:16–17). And God sends the Holy Spirit to guide us (see 1 Thess. 4:8). This example also reminds us that to discern the divine message in a Scripture text, we need to take in its totality rather than focus intently on a particular word or phrase.

Finally, it's worth noting that in closing this letter, Paul used the Greek phase: *ho hos kalōn hymas*, which translates to: "the one who calls you" (1 Thess. 5:24a). This Greek phrase conveys the sense of a continuous action. Paul, then and now, reminds each and every Christian that God's call to the mission of faithfulness and evangelization is ongoing. It is not a singular event.

THREE

✠ ✠ ✠

THE LETTER TO THE GALATIANS

3.1 SOME BACKGROUND

Paul passed through Galatia on his second missionary journey and again on his third, and he likely wrote his letter to the Galatians during his several-year stay at Ephesus during his third missionary journey. The new Christians whom Paul was addressing in Galatia were mostly converts from paganism. They were now being enticed by other "Christian missionaries" to add the observances of the Jewish law, including the rite of circumcision, to the Cross of Christ as a means of salvation.

These "missionaries" were seriously undermining Paul's teaching authority, asserting that he had not been trained by Jesus Himself, that his gospel did not agree with that of the original and "true" apostles in Jerusalem, and that he had kept from his converts in Galatia the necessity of accepting circumcision and following other key obligations of the Jewish law. And so in this letter, Paul defended his apostolic authority and offered the Galatians correct understandings of the Faith.

This letter, written about 54 AD, also gives Paul's own account of how he came to faith.

The principal divisions of this letter are:

✠ Address (1:1–5)

✠ Loyalty to the Gospel (1:6–10)

✠ Defense of His Gospel and Authority (1:11–2:21)

✠ Faith and Liberty (3:1–4:31)

✠ Exhortation to Christian Living (5:1–6:10)

✠ Conclusion (6:11–18)

3.2 FREEDOM FROM THE LAW

In this letter to the Galatians, Paul used the Koine Greek word *nomos*, which is usually translated into English as "the law," twenty-five times. The word *nomos* meant "that which is assigned." But it also had two quite different meanings to Jews, and the listener needed to discern from the context which meaning was intended:[26]

1. the Decalogue (the Ten Commandments), which is found in the portion of Jewish Scripture known in Hebrew as the Torah.

2. the Mosaic Law, the means of defining the terms of loyalty to God. This meant the *mitzvot* ("commandments"),[27] which were then interpreted by the Pharisees and were regarded as the "hedge around the Torah." This tradition of interpretation seems to have at times contradicted the actual written text, as Jesus chastised the Pharisees with: "You nullify the word of God in favor of your tradition that you have handed on" (Mark 7:13).

These conflicting meanings of "the law" led to an internal struggle most Jews wrestled with: by observing "the law," was one striving

---

[26] Marrow, *Paul: His Letters and His Theology.*

[27] Over a thousand years after the birth of Christ, the Jewish rabbi Maimonides defined and set the number of *mitzvot* at 613.

to do the will of God, or was one striving to secure God's favor? To pagans, the answer was clear: it was currying favor. The Roman expression for this was *do ut des*, which meant, "I give that you may give back."

It's evident from Paul's letter that the Galatians were being misled by the teaching that a man was justified by his "works of the law." The term "works of the law" meant the rituals of the *mitzvot*. Paul's response to the Galatians was "I do not nullify the grace of God; for if justification comes through the law, then Christ died for nothing" (Gal. 2:21). One is not "saved by the law" (performing the *mitzvot*) but through faith in Christ. Unfortunately, many today mistake the statement in Galatians 2:21 to mean that one is saved by faith alone.

During Paul's lifetime, Christianity was still a sect within Judaism, much like the Essenes and Zealots. Back then, Christians first attended synagogue and then went to someone's home for a service known as the "Breaking of the Bread" (what is today known as the Eucharist). So Paul had many opponents in Galatia who insisted that adhering to all the "observances" of Judaism, including the rituals of the *mitzvot* and circumcision, were required of all Christians. In a similar fashion, Paul's opponents in Philippi insisted that adhering to all the "observances" of Judaism was the pathway to perfection. And in Corinth, adherence to the Jewish *mitzvot* was regarded as the pathway to "wisdom."[28]

One might ask, "Why were people so drawn to 'works of the law?'" Because there is a need in all of us for reassurance in

---

[28] This attitude in Corinth may show the beginnings of Gnosticism in the Christian Church — the idea that one needed secret knowledge in order to be saved. In the letters attributed to Paul, after his imprisonment in Rome, we will see considerable attention to the issue of Gnosticism infiltrating the Christian communities.

where we stand in our relationship with God, just as children seek reassurance from their parents. Paul's opponents were playing on this weakness.

To Paul, at its root, ""the law"" (here meaning Decalogue) is God-given. That law made known the roots of sin which led to death and then to the saving grace of Christ. To Paul, the price a Jew paid for "freedom from the law" (here meaning the rituals of *mitzvot*) was to "die to the law." That is, the Jewish people would have to give up the satisfaction they had felt from faithfully expressing loyalty to God through the *mitzvot*. The rituals of the *mitzvot* were regarded as making the "observer" more pleasing to God as he or she ensured divine help and protection. And so Paul's teachings had enormous importance to Jews, but they also threatened the "good news" of the gospel for them. But this teaching had no importance at all to Gentiles, who knew no Decalogue or the rituals of the *mitzvot* and who had no experience of gaining favor with the gods; their religious practices had all been about appeasing the gods.

Paul said to the Galatians, "For through the law I died to the law, that I might live for God" (Gal. 2:19). No number of rituals will gain salvation; salvation has been freely given by God. Our part is to accept it by keeping the commandments of the Decalogue, which Paul believed was God-given (see Gal. 3:21). That law made known the sin that led to death, but it also revealed the saving grace of Christ.

Paul found that drawing the Jews away from the seduction of the rituals of the *mitzvot* was as difficult as drawing the Gentiles away from the worship of their favorite false god. Although an idol is inanimate, something visible is more reassuring than an invisible God. Likewise, living by prescribed actions is more reassuring than trusting in One who asks little in return. We tend to make what is asked of us much greater than it actually is. Recall Eve's exaggeration of God's command about the fruit of the Tree of Knowledge: "you shall not eat it *or even touch it*, or else you will die" (Gen. 3:3).[29]

3.3 VICTIMS OF WITCHCRAFT

We have seen how the people of Galatia were being misled by some opponents of Paul whose teachings were contrary to what Paul had taught, and so Paul heightened the dangers of these false teachings by writing that the Galatians were victims of witchcraft, the practice of invoking spirits to gain advantage over people: "O stupid Galatians! Who has bewitched you, before whose eyes Jesus Christ was publicly portrayed as crucified?" (Gal. 3:1)

First-century Jews and Christians believed that forces of Evil were everywhere, so the practice of witchcraft was quite common. It's almost certain that Paul's opponents would have accused him of engaging in witchcraft, just as the Pharisees had done to Jesus: "This man drives out demons only by the power of Beelzebub, the prince of demons" (Matt. 12:24; cf. Mark 3:22b and Luke 11:15). By invoking the enemies of God, those who practiced witchcraft were considered enemies of the people. Indeed, one who invoked the power of Beelzebub was regarded as guilty of treason.

To be a victim of witchcraft was considered to be the ultimate misfortune. Victims were therefore motivated to expose the culprits. Paul uses this aspect of ancient Jewish culture to rally the community in Galatia in ridding itself of the "false brothers" (Gal. 2:4a) who were exercising ill-gotten influence over them and who were teaching false ideas.

---

[29] God's actual command to Adam and Eve in Genesis 2:16–17 lacked any reference to touching the tree: "You are free to eat from any of the trees of the garden except the tree of knowledge of good and evil. From that tree you shall not eat; when you eat from it you shall die."

3.4 Redemption

In this letter, we see the early stages of Paul's explanation of the redemption brought by Jesus Christ. The subject would get much deeper treatment in his letter a few years later to the Romans.

> Paul said to the Galatians:
>
> When the fullness of time had come, God sent his Son, born of a woman, born under the law, to ransom those under the law, so that we might receive adoption. As proof that you are children, God sent the spirit of his Son into our hearts, crying out, "Abba, Father!" (Gal. 4:4–6)

There are five important details in this statement that need to be considered carefully:[30]

1. "born of a woman": that is, entered the world as a human being, not solely as a divine creature.
2. "born under the law": that is, as a Jew under the covenant with Moses (which Paul asserted ended with Christ's death).
3. "to ransom those under the law": that is, to pay the debt owed by mankind, who failed to faithfully keep the covenant with Moses. This phrase was the basis of what later became known as "Vicarious Satisfaction" — the concept that Jesus underwent grave punishment and death on behalf of us to appease the Father, who then responded to us with mercy and salvation. By the time of his letter to the Romans, Paul would see the

[30] Morrow, Ibid.

shortcoming in this idea[31] and articulate to the Romans the "Ultimate Gift of Love" explanation of Jesus' redemptive act. This is a good example of the Holy Spirit working in the life of Paul.

4. "receive adoption": that is, accepting full care and responsibility for our (spiritual) survival. In the ancient world, every child needed to be adopted. When a child was born, the infant was not part of the family until a male, biological father or not, claimed the child as his own and gave the infant a name. At that point, the male became the infant's father and accepted full care and responsibility for the child's survival. If no male "adopted" the child in this manner, then the midwife placed the infant in a large clay pot and abandoned him or her by the roadside.[32]

5. "spirit of the Son": Paul used "spirit," or "spirit of the Son," or "spirit of the Father" or "spirit of the Lord" 139 times in his letters as he tried to articulate what the animating and empowering force was that baptized Christians received. We have come to understand this as being the Holy Spirit. It is from Luke, as well as the later letters written on Paul's behalf of or in his name, that we find the term "Holy Spirit" used even more widely.

[31] If God forgives our sins, then there is no further debt to be paid. We may have to make amends for the effects of our sins, but there remains no debt to God. Purgatory is not for punishment, it is for "purification, so as to achieve the holiness necessary to enter the joy of heaven" (CCC 1030).

[32] J. E. Boswell, "Exposition and Oblation: The Abandonment of Children and the Ancient and Medieval Family," in American Historical Review (Oxford: Oxford University Press, 1984).

3.5 The "Good News"

When Paul spoke of "proclaiming the gospel," he used the Koine Greek word *evangelio* (gospel) to mean the "good news" of Jesus Christ, not the texts that would later be called the Gospels. The Gospels had not even been written during Paul's lifetime. Paul taught that the "good news" of Jesus Christ was that we are redeemed (that is, brought back to where we belong with access to eternal life with God) through Jesus' Passion and death, not through anything we have done. Our reassurance is that our relationship with God has been set right through Christ (see Gal. 3:26). There is no means of earning salvation, only accepting it. Therefore, we keep the Ten Commandments because we are saved, not that we might be saved. Sadly, many continue to strive after recognition in the sight of God, not realizing that we are already granted all the recognition we need (see Gal. 4:7).

3.6 Some Other Insights

As noted earlier, order was of the utmost importance to the people of Paul's time, even the ordering of time itself. Much of the discourse in chapters 3 and 4 of this letter, which concern the covenant with Moses and the covenant with Abraham, is better understood if we recognize that for Paul, the moment of transition from "old time" (covenant of the law) to "new time" (covenant of faith and love) was the death of Christ on the Cross (see Gal. 3:13–14). Man's "old" relationship with God (obedience earns love) came from the Torah; man's "new" relationship with God (love engenders obedience) came from Christ's death on the Cross, for Christ's sacrifice restored man's access to eternal life with God. When Paul wrote about this access to eternal life with God, he used the Greek word *dikaiosyne*,[33] which is sometimes translated as "righteousness" and sometimes as "justification," as in Galatians 3:11. *Dikaiosyne* was the unquestionable aim of all religious behavior, and it did not come from the law but only came from faith and God's grace (see Gal. 2:21). Paul understood that Christ's salvific act fulfilled the covenant with Abraham and ended the covenant with Moses. For this reason, the death of Christ on the Cross was Paul's demarcation point between "old" and "new" time.[34] So to Paul, those who continued to live on the old side of that boundary were therefore "disordered" and "unholy" (however, we should note that being "unholy" did not necessarily imply being sinful).

The Gentiles likewise had a strong sense of need for social order, yet they had no concept of sin, so Paul framed his early definitions of sin to be in terms of violations of society's (and therefore God's) laws. And so in Galatians 5:18–21, Paul's condemnation of "works of the flesh" closely reflected the Ten Commandments. Transgressions against these laws would cause the loss of access to eternal life with God, as Paul concluded this passage with the warning: "those who do such things will not inherit the kingdom of God" (Gal. 5:21). "Kingdom of God" here is a translation of the Greek term *basileian theou*, which had a different meaning than what we encounter in the Gospels. In his letter to the Galatians, Paul was referring to Heaven, whereas the Gospel meaning is "a way of living in which Christ reigns

---

[33] The Greek word *dikaiosyne* literally meant to be delivered from a deserved punishment.

[34] Since October 1582, however, the modern world has taken the position (by adopting the Gregorian Calendar) that the transition from "old" (referred to as BC or Before Christ) to "new" (referred to as AD or Anno Domini) was the birth of Christ, not His death.

in the hearts of believers as they strive to fulfill the will of God in this life. It separates us from the kingdom of the world and the devil."[35]

Paul's focus on social order and "old" and "new" time may seem odd or a bit extreme to us today, but Paul's first listeners shared a worldview that was very dualistic (Good vs. Evil; Spirit vs, Flesh; even covenant with Abraham vs covenant with Moses). Remember that Paul saw not only false teachers but Evil itself attacking and polluting his church communities. In Paul's thinking, there was no ambiguity between who was "in" and who was "out." Therefore, an important ritual Paul engaged in, as part of his teaching, was boundary identification, building, and maintenance, as at this point in the evolution of Christian communities, it appears that there were few workable techniques for resolving conflicts. We will see that change considerably as we progress through Paul's letters.

[35] Hugh Pope, "Kingdom of God," in *The Catholic Encyclopedia* (New York: Robert Appleton Company, 1910).

FOUR

✠ ✠ ✠

THE LETTER TO PHILEMON

4.1 SOME BACKGROUND

This short letter was addressed to Philemon, the head of a house-church in Colossae, to his wife Apphia, to someone named Archippus, and to the "church" at Philemon's house. It's believed to have been written by Paul while he was in prison in Ephesus around 55 AD.

Prior to the destruction of the Temple in 70 AD and the expulsion of Christians from the synagogue, Christianity was part of Judaism. As noted earlier, Christians first attended synagogue and then retired to someone's house for the Breaking of the Bread ceremony (now called the Eucharist). This was presided over by the *presbyteros* ("elder" or "presbyter"), the head-of-household. This is the origins of the Christian priesthood. It's fairly clear that Philemon was a presbyter.

This letter concerns Onesimus, a slave from Colossae who had run away from his master and who was perhaps guilty of theft in the process. It appears that Philemon was his master. Onesimus was converted to Christ by Paul, and Paul was sending him back to his master, with this letter, asking that he be welcomed willingly, not just as a slave but as a brother in Christ. This reconciliation would restore order in the house of Philemon by having Onesimus returned to his "proper place."

This letter consists of only one chapter.

4.2 SLAVERY IN PAUL'S TIME

Under Mosaic Law, every Hebrew household was entitled to a plot of land in fulfillment of God's promise: "to your descendants I will give this land" (Gen. 12:7). In principle, land in Israel could not be sold, but in practice, land was frequently lost through foreclosure on a debt. The most common reasons for incurring debt were crop failure and inability to pay taxes, which were an enormous economic burden under the Roman Empire. A wealthy neighbor would loan a poorer neighbor the money, but the loan was secured by the debtor's land and the labor of the members of the debtor's household.

When a household defaulted, which was very common, the creditor foreclosed on the land, and those in the debtor's household became "indentured," or debt-slaves, to the creditor. (In the Roman Empire, there were also forced-labor slaves who were prisoners of war, but these people were the property of the Empire, not individual households). A debt could be paid off or forgiven prior to foreclosure, but unfortunately, this rarely happened, and foreclosure usually led to indentured servitude, or debt-slavery, for generations to come. It is estimated that in the first century, one in five persons in the Roman Empire was an indentured servant, or debt-slave.[36]

Because it was unlawful for a Hebrew to enslave another Hebrew, they referred to debt-slaves as "servants" (Lev. 25:35). Since these people were racially identical to their masters, these "servants" were marked by a symbol of shame: large earrings or "tags of ownership"

---

[36] "Slavery in the Roman World," in *Ancient History Encyclopedia* (Horsham, UK: World History Encyclopedia Ltd., 2013).

(see Exod. 21:6). These "servants" were slaves in every sense of the word, except they could not be physically abused and were paid wages (see Deut. 24:14–15), and they were allowed to celebrate the Hebrew holidays with the master's household (see Deut. 12:18). In addition, under Hebrew law, debt-slaves were to be released every Sabbatical Year (each seventh year on the Hebrew calendar). However, any children born during their servitude, as well as a wife who might have been provided by the creditor, "belonged" to the creditor and were known as *vernae*.

The debt-slave no longer owned any land and therefore no longer "shared in the promise" and was termed a "stranger in the land." Even upon their release, former debtors often had no means of support, and so they frequently exercised their "right" (see Exod. 21:1–6) to remain as a servant in the master's household. All debt-slaves ("servants") were property, and they passed from father to sons via inheritance. Thus, debt was a pit into which a whole household might fall and remain for generations, until perhaps they were freed as part of a creditor's will or as a magnanimous gesture.

4.3 EMBRACING THE NEW ORDER

For a very long time, Western scholars were puzzled over why Philemon's community, and later the larger Christian community, preserved this letter. On the surface, it appears to be a personal correspondence addressing a purely private concern. Clearly, at some point, this letter was shared with the community that gathered at Philemon's house. And that community must have seen something of great significance *to themselves* in what Paul had written. But what?

It was not until biblical scholars came to know more about the role of *pietas* in the Middle East and Paul's addressing Philemon (see Philem. 1:7, 20) and Onesimus (see Philem. 1:16) as *brother* that it became evident as to why this letter was treasured and later became part of the canon of the New Testament. *Pietas* is Latin for *loyalty*, and we in the West generally derive our idea of piety and loyalty from the Romans. To them, piety was a solemn duty to the gods, to country, and to family. It was even touted on some of their coins.[37] But to Middle Easterners, piety had a much deeper more personal meaning. It did not relate principally to the gods or the country. Rather it was the profound responsibility each person had for the care and guidance of each member of their extended family.

In the ancient Middle East, family came before all else. In their communities, there was no police force. Each extended family was responsible for the proper conduct of its members, and the larger community relied on them to meet that responsibility. There was also no social security system; each extended family was responsible for caring for its members, even those who no longer lived at home.[38]

In the ancient Middle East, for one to refer to another as *brother* or *sister* was not an expression of endearment or camaraderie. Rather, it was an affirmation that the person was considered a member of the speaker's extended family, blood relative or not. It was an affirmation that they shared the responsibilities of piety to one another.

Throughout his ministry, Paul taught that Baptism was much more than an induction ritual into Christianity. Rather, Baptism up ends the whole prevailing social order. Each person is born into the world without access to eternal life with God as a consequence of Original Sin. In Baptism, each person dies to his former self and rises in new life. All the baptized receive the very same divine gift of this new life. Therefore, all the distinctions between persons that

[37] T. Christopher Hoklotubbe, *Civilized Piety: The Rhetoric of Pietas in the Pastoral Epistles and the Roman Empire*, (Waco, Texas: Baylor University Press, 2017}.

[38] *Pietas* persists to this day in much of the Middle East. There, the extended family is known as the *hamula*.

may prevail in the larger world, such as master/slave, rich/poor, and Jew/Gentile, have no place among the baptized. All are equal. And all share the obligations of piety to one another.

Every baptized Christian is a brother or sister in Christ. Every Christian must embrace that new order, willingly accepting the duties of piety to one another. This is the reality about which Paul was reminding Philemon, and the larger community, in his letter. Since Onesimus was baptized, Philemon and the whole community were to receive Onesimus as a brother. While the master/slave distinction may prevail in the larger world around them, that distinction must have no place among baptized Christians.

4.4 SOME OTHER INSIGHTS

Paul was well aware that Christianity brought with it a need for a very different worldview than what currently prevailed. And that transformation would take considerable time. It is in this context that Paul was trying, in this letter, to work out the religious reality that in the Christian community setting, there was no distinction between Philemon (master) and Onesimus (slave), but in the larger cultural world setting, there still existed a sharp distinction between them that focused intently on things being in "proper order."

FIVE

✠ ✠ ✠

THE FIRST LETTER TO
THE CORINTHIANS

5.1 SOME BACKGROUND

Paul established a Christian community in Corinth about the year 51 AD, on his second missionary journey. The city, a commercial crossroads, was a melting pot of devotees from various pagan cults, and it was marked by a measure of moral depravity that was not unusual in a great seaport. When Paul departed from the city, he left the eloquent Apollos, a Jewish Christian originally from Alexandria, in charge, who rendered great service to the community and whose labors were generously acknowledge by Paul in his letter (see 1 Cor. 3:5–8).[39]

While Paul was in Ephesus on his third missionary journey, he received a letter from the Corinthians with troubling news about their city, including scandalous behavior among some of their community leaders. Paul therefore wrote this letter from Ephesus, around the year 56 AD, as a response to the Corinthians' wide spectrum of issues. This letter provides us with a fuller insight into the life of a

---

[39] Some scholars believe that it was Apollos who wrote the Letter to the Hebrews.

first-generation Christian community than any other text in the New Testament. We know that Paul had already written at least one other letter to Corinth (see 1 Cor. 5:9), but that letter has not survived.

The principal divisions of this letter are:

✠ Address (1:1–9)
✠ Disorders in Corinthian Community (1:10–6:20)
✠ Answers to the Corinthians' Questions (7:1–11:1)
✠ Problems in Liturgical Assemblies (11:2–14:40)
✠ The Resurrection (15:1–58)
✠ Conclusion (16:1–24)

5.2 LIMITS ON FREEDOM

Paul sought to encourage those unnamed people who were scandalizing the community to reject their immoral behavior and to renew their commitment to a life grounded in the love of Christ (see 1 Cor. 10:6–13). The "good news" brought freedom from "works of the law," but that responsibility commanded a price — personal accountability. We are not to separate ourselves from the world, we are rather to separate ourselves from those who do evil (see 1 Cor. 5:13). Tolerating them does not help them or the community.

Here, Paul was promoting excommunication. Excommunication was, and still is, the ritual by which a community separates themselves from those whose conduct scandalizes or otherwise harms the community. Excommunication, or "unbinding," was common in Judaism. Their cultural focus on separating that which did not belong together as a means of imitating God carried over into early Christianity. To this day, excommunication is not a punishment, it is a means of protecting the community; and it is also a call to the offenders to realize the error of their ways. Excommunication is lifted for a repentant offender; it is not intended to be permanent. The

Christian principle of "bringing back our erring brothers" has displaced many excommunications, except in the most egregious cases.

5.3 MEAT SACRIFICED TO IDOLS

Greco-Roman society was saturated with idol worship, and it was common for meat sold in the marketplace to have been consecrated as a sacrifice to pagan gods prior to its sale. The Jews would have nothing to do with such meat, believing that to partake of such "consecrated" meat was to give tacit approval of idol worship—kind of a second-hand idolatry. Most Gentiles rejected the notion that such meat was tainted, and they held that they could eat meat sacrificed to idols without endorsing idolatry—they had not actually offered the sacrifice, after all. The matter had become a big point of contention within the Corinthian Christian community.[40]

Paul pointed out that his audience all knew that "an idol has no real existence" (1 Cor. 8:4, RSVCE). Therefore, to "sacrifice" something to idols was meaningless. But then he said that while their knowledge was true, in partaking of meat sacrificed to idols, one might give a misleading example to those with lesser knowledge, and they might be led astray as a result (see 1 Cor. 8:9–11). Paul contended that as a practical matter, our freedom was limited by what may mislead or scandalize others. Christian freedom thus has a self-sacrificing price: we are called to adapt our actions for the benefit of "the brother for whom Christ died" (1 Cor. 8:11).

5.4 MARRIAGE AND DIVORCE

Chapter 7 of Paul's First Letter to the Corinthians is perhaps one of the most argued about texts in the New Testament. On first reading,

---

[40] Ben Witherington III, *A Week in the Life of Corinth* (Westmont, IL: InterVarsity Press, 2012).

Paul's advice on marriage seems almost outrageous. So to understand Paul's advice on marriage and divorce, we need to take into account the cultural setting in which he was giving that advice.

First, the backdrop: Jews "understood" marriage very differently than did Gentiles. Jews married for the purpose of procreation: they were following God's command to "be fertile and multiply" (Gen. 1:28a). As a practical matter, children had always been the "unpaid labor" contributing to the support of the family. Even in urban settings, children were regarded as essential to the survival of the family.[41] However, marriage among Gentiles was largely a matter of inheritance strategy and social responsibility. One married for the benefit of sustaining order in the community, not for procreation—children were the result of sexual pleasure. Every city had their own laws governing marriage. As a general rule, a female was not an adult until she was married. If a man was not married by the age of thirty-five, he suffered the loss of his civil rights. A Gentile man could only have one wife at a time, but it was normal to have several concubines.[42]

As noted earlier, in the mid-first century, Christians were convinced that Jesus' return would be "any day now"—the Imminent *Parousia*. Paul also was convinced of the Imminent *Parousia* (see 1 Cor. 7:26, 29, 31). Since they believed that the world would be ending very soon, they therefore thought that it would be irresponsible to enter into marriage and bring into the world children who would never even reach the age of reason, let alone "contribute" to the family. Even people who were already married would be seen as irresponsible if they were to have more children. And while overall

[41] Fr. Donald Senior et al., eds., "Reading Guide to 1 Corinthians," in *The Catholic Study Bible* (Oxford: Oxford University Press, 1990).

[42] *Elaine Fantham et al., Women in the Classical World (Oxford: Oxford University Press, 1994).*

there was considerable moral depravity in Corinth, some in the Corinthian Christian community argued that sex itself, even in marriage, was giving in to man's basest instincts and was therefore wrong (see 1 Cor. 7:28).

It was in this context that Paul did not promote people getting married or having children. Paul encouraged marital abstinence where it was "doable" (see 1 Cor. 7:1–9). But Paul was clearly not against marriage; he was deeply convinced that sex in marriage, properly regarded, was a self-giving to another, the very core of Christian spirituality. But the overriding consideration of his original audience was the expected near-term end of the world. And so we see why it is so important to understand the cultural context in which Paul was writing, or else we can seriously misinterpret his advice.

On the subject of divorce, Paul was often confronted with the problem of a married Gentile couple in which one spouse converted to Christianity and the other did not. In the Gentile world, men freely divorced and remarried. But the Christian prohibition against divorce and remarriage applied to both parties equally (see 1 Cor. 7:10–11). Paul taught that if two unbelievers married and then one converted to Christianity and the unbeliever left the believer, then the Christian, who had been abandoned by the unbeliever, was not to be condemned to a life of unwanted celibacy; in this case, the Christian believer could properly enter into a new marriage (see 1 Cor. 7:15). This is the basis for what is known today as the "Pauline Privilege."

5.5 UNDERSTANDING THE "LAST SUPPER"

The term "Last Supper" was adopted by Catholics in the sixteenth century, when the Reformists insisted on calling it the "Lord's Supper," the term Paul used (see 1 Cor. 11:20b). From Paul's letter, it's clear that the Corinthians were combining the "Breaking of the

Bread" service (now called "Eucharist") with their communal meal and calling it the "Lord's Supper." Unfortunately, the communal meal tended to separate the "haves" from the "have-nots," making the experience humiliating for those who were less affluent.

The word *Eucharist* comes from the Greek word *eucharistein*, which means to give thanks for a freely-given gift. In this letter to the Corinthians, Paul presented the first written account of the "Words of Institution of the Eucharist":

> For I received from the Lord what I also handed on to you, that the Lord Jesus, on the night he was handed over, took bread, and, after he had given thanks, broke it and said, "This is my body that is for you. Do this in remembrance of me." In the same way also the cup, after supper, saying, "This cup is the new covenant in my blood. Do this, as often as you drink it, in remembrance of me." For as often as you eat this bread and drink the cup, you proclaim the death of the Lord until he comes. (1 Cor. 11:23–26)

In this passage, the Greek word *anamnesis*, which is translated above as "remembrance," actually meant "make present again."

Paul then admonished the Corinthians that the Eucharist was sacred and therefore must be treated with great reverence. What is sacred must be kept separate from the ordinary. Furthermore:

> Therefore, whoever eats the bread or drinks the cup of the Lord unworthily will have to answer for the body and blood of the Lord. A person should examine himself, and so eat the bread and

drink the cup. For anyone who eats and drinks without discerning the body eats and drinks judgment on himself. (1 Cor. 11:27–29)

5.6 MEANING OF "CHURCH"

Paul addressed this letter "to the church (*ekklesia*) that is in Corinth" (1 Cor 1:2). He then spoke of *ekklesia* (normally translated as church) numerous times throughout the letter. (e.g. 1 Cor 6:4; 10:32; 11:16, 18. 22; 14:4, 12, 23; 15:9; 16:19). The meaning of "church," as used in this and in Paul's other letters, has been something that Christians have argued about ever since the Reformation. The Koine Greek word *ekklesia* meant a "called community." The approximate Hebrew term was *qahal Yahweh*, which means "household of God." In the letters attributed to Paul, *ekklesia*, which is generally translated into English as "church," was used in two ways:

1. Paul had appointed bishops and presbyters, and we know there were deacons, so a clergy existed in Paul's time to provide cohesion to a federation of house-churches. Recall that Christians first went to the synagogue, then to house-churches (private homes) for the Breaking of the Bread (Eucharist), which was presided over by a presbyter, who was often assisted by at least one deacon. (There were no parishes as we know them today.) A major city or large geographic area was referred to as an *ekklesia* (church), and it was headed by a bishop. This was the equivalent of what is known today as a diocese. Therefore, "church" was a federation of house-churches in a city or geographic area. The Church in Corinth and the Church in Ephesus are examples.

2. In the letter to the Ephesians, however, *ekklesia* (church) clearly meant the entire called community of believers, "the Body of Christ," because they all partook of the Body of Christ in the Eucharist, and "we become what we consume."[43] They were all one in their common beliefs and unity in Christ.

Today, the word "church" continues to have a dual meaning: the communal unit (parish and its worship space) or the organizational unit (those with common beliefs and their teaching and doctrinal hierarchy). One must discern from context which meaning is intended. The communal unit is often implied when "church" is spelled with a lowercase "c", while an uppercase "C" often implies the organizational unit.

The reason for the controversy over the meaning of "church" is that Reformers argued that the original federation of house-churches is the only "true church" that Christ intended and that Paul preached. They argued that the organizational unit of those with common beliefs and their teachings and hierarchy was a "much later invention." The Reformers contended that the Letter to the Ephesians does not represent "Paul's teachings." But we need to keep in mind that the Letter to the Ephesians is a part of the inspired Word of God. And we are guided by the entirety of the inspired Word of God, not specifically "Paul's teachings" per se.

When we later consider more closely the Letter to the Ephesians, we will find that the argument that the hierarchical organization does not represent Paul's teachings is not as compelling as it might sound at first. As we progress through Paul's letters we'll see that, to him, "church" was fundamentally a community called to worship

---

[43] Mary H. Allies, *The Best of Augustine: Selections from the Writings of St Augustine of Hippo* (London: Burns and Oates, 2016).

Christ as Lord and celebrate the Lord's Supper (the Eucharist) as the Body of Christ. The organization of such a community is a matter of order, not a matter of purpose for being.

5.7 MEANING OF "GRACE"

Sometimes, Paul used the Greek word, *charis* (which is usually translated as "grace") to mean the gift resulting from the death of Christ: renewed access to eternal life.[44] This can be confusing for modern listeners, because the word "grace" is normally taken today to mean that which brings about or sustains holiness in us and which aids us in particular actions in our life (see *CCC* 1996–2005). *Charis* originally meant "favor." Grace is, of course, a freely-given gift, or favor, but when Paul used the word in the context of Christ's suffering and death, he meant the specific God-given gift of access to eternal life (e.g. 1 Cor. 1:4; 3:10; 15:10).

5.8 CHARISMS OF THE HOLY SPIRIT

It is evident from Paul's letter that there were far too many in Corinth who saw themselves as being "gifted" with leadership ability. So Paul instructed them on spiritual gifts, or charisms (Greek *charismata*). Paul taught that one does not decide his or her charisms; they are spiritual gifts of the Holy Spirit. One must, however, discern their charism(s). All charisms are for the benefit of others.

> There are different kinds of spiritual gifts [*charismata*] but the same Spirit; there are different forms of service but the same Lord; there are different workings but the same God who produces all of them in everyone. To each

[44] Marrow, *Paul: His Letters and His Theology.*

individual, the manifestation of the Spirit is
given for some benefit. To one is given through
the Spirit the *expression of wisdom* [the ability to
apply moral principles to everyday situations];
to another the *expression of knowledge* according
to the same Spirit [the ability to intuitively discern patterns and cause-effect relationships]; to
another *faith* by the same Spirit [the ability to
be confident in what is hoped for and assured of
what is unseen]; to another *gifts of healing* by
the one Spirit [the ability to help others become
whole and well]; to another *mighty deeds* [the
ability to do what appears to be hopeless or cannot be done]; to another *prophecy* [the ability to
speak in an inspired way with conviction that
transcends the ordinary]; to another *discernment
of spirits* [the ability to perceive and distinguish
good from bad]; to another *varieties of tongues*
[the ability to convey thoughts and feelings in a
moving and convincing way]; to another *interpretation of tongues* [the ability to understand
and explain the actions and motives of others].
But one and the same Spirit produces all of
these, distributing them individually to each
person as he wishes. (1 Cor. 12:4–11)

It is essential that each of us realizes that discerning and applying
the charisms we receive from the Holy Spirit is the main path for
us in spreading the "good news" of Jesus Christ. Our charisms are
the instruments of evangelization that reveal Jesus through us to
others and render His presence tangible in the world. We are agents

of God's purpose in the world, channels of his love, truth, and healing for others. This is our God-given mission.

As Paul noted, charisms are gifts of the Holy Spirit (*CCC* 799), and the Holy Spirit is poured out in fullness in Baptism. In the sacrament of Confirmation, we are "sealed with the gifts of the Holy Spirit," and we formally accept the gifts. To be "sealed" is to receive an identifying mark—our distinctive charism becomes the visible means by which, through our words and actions, we reveal Christ to the world.[45]

5.9 FAITH AND THE RESURRECTION OF JESUS

As a Pharisee, Paul had initially believed in the Jewish expectation of the resurrection from the dead, which by the first century, was that "the resurrection" would involve a restoration of the nation of Israel, not of each individual person. Some people would benefit from the fact that the resurrection took place, but there was no common agreement on how they would benefit. Would they actually come back to life? Or was some other benefit in store for them? And so the ultimate reward for a Jew was to be part of the "righteous" at the resurrection. They had no concept of having eternal life with God. Furthermore, the Jewish people understood salvation and redemption in a different way than we understand the terms today: "salvation" meant being saved from oppression by others, such as the Romans, while "redemption" meant to be restored to where one belongs, or former prosperity.

But in "knowing" Christ, Paul came to understand the resurrection very differently, and his new faith also profoundly realigned his understanding of both salvation and redemption.

---

[45] In Paul's time, Baptism, Confirmation, and First Eucharist were experienced as one sacrament, called the Sacrament of Initiation. It was only in later times that they became known as three separate sacraments.

Christians believe in individual bodily resurrection into eternal life because Christ Himself was bodily resurrected into eternal life. As Paul put it: "If there is no resurrection of the dead, then neither has Christ been raised. And if Christ has not been raised, then empty [too] is our preaching; empty, too, your faith" (1 Cor. 15:13–14). In that passage, Paul used the Koine Greek word, *pistos*, which is translated as "faith" or "trust" (see also 1 Cor. 4:2), to mean holding to a spiritual truth that is not amenable to physical proof.

With this understanding of Jesus' Resurrection, then, believers are not saved from oppression by others but from the consequence of sin — death. They are redeemed by being brought back to where they belong, sharing eternal life with God. And they are restored to the prosperity of being children of God, heirs through Jesus Christ.

5.10 SOME OTHER INSIGHTS

In this letter, we again see the influence of the first-century Jewish worldview. For example, Paul defines sin as violation of God's "law," but this violation is more of a reflection of the great cosmic struggle than a personal failure. In our times, we usually regard temptation by the devil as the principal spiritual threat to us. We see the struggle between Good and Evil being fought in the heart of each person, but we rarely, if ever, see the struggle in a cosmic sense.

But to Paul and his first audience, the whole order of faith was being subverted by the chaos of error, and the stakes were very high. To see this, we need to compare the passage we previously considered in Galatians, which read, "those who do such things will not inherit the kingdom of God" (Gal. 5:21), with one from this letter: "Do you not know that the unjust will not inherit the kingdom of God?" (1 Cor. 6:9).

In Galatians, Paul characterized sinners as wrong-doers who would lose out on eternal life with God. But in this letter, sinners were the *adikoi* ("unjust"), a word which usually referred to a corrupt judge who was lacking in fairness and impartiality, one who sided with the "bad" against the "good." So in this context, to sin was to "throw in" with the wrong side in the cosmic Good vs. Evil struggle.[46]

God may deal with violations of His "law" in a variety of ways, including patience, slowness to judge, time for repentance. In Paul's day, the perception of sin as corruption demanded more immediate action. Either the offending behavior was promptly stopped, or the offender was to be separated from the community.

---

[46] Some English Bibles translate the Greek word *adikoi* as "unrighteous" rather than "unjust," but this loses the Good vs. Evil struggle connotation Paul was after, an idea his first listeners would have readily identified with.

SIX

✠ ✠ ✠

THE SECOND LETTER TO
THE CORINTHIANS

6.1 SOME BACKGROUND

This "letter" appears to be a collection of fragments of what were six letters (in this approximate order) written from Ephesus around 57–58 AD:

1. First letter: 2:14–6:13 and 7:2–4
2. Second letter: chapters 10–13
3. Third letter: chapter 8
4. Fourth letter: chapter 9
5. Fifth letter: 1:1–2:13 and 7:5–16
6. Sixth letter: 6:14–7:1 (this appears to be a non-Pauline addition made at the time the fragments were collected)

It's evident from this letter that Paul's opponents in Corinth had preached a very watered-down version of Christianity and had prompted much anger against Paul for "complicating" their message. The opposition to Paul was well coordinated, and his opponents came with what they claimed were "letters of recommendation." They offered "simplified truths" and a property-based membership in the community. Their liturgies were very theatrical in style and substance, and they berated Paul for being too dull and unimaginative. There was no mention of "take up your cross," no mention of "love your enemies," no mention of the redemptive nature of suffering.

As the Corinthians were beset by all kinds of teachings that were contrary to what Paul had taught, Paul's missive to them was, basically, that the world of true Christians was upside-down: the humble are not the inferior, the weak are not the losers, the helpless are not the defeated, and the Christ who was crucified lives on in glory. Perhaps no other "letter" evokes so vividly the image of the trials and sufferings of early Christian life and Paul's opposition from "false apostles." The letter fragments, as they have been assembled, lay out lessons in the realities of Christian living.[47]

The principal divisions in the resulting document are:

- ✠ Address (1:1–11)
- ✠ Crisis between Paul and the Corinthians (1:12–7:16)
- ✠ The Collection for Jerusalem (8:1–9:15)
- ✠ Paul's Defense of His Ministry (10:1–13:10)
- ✠ Conclusion (13:11–13)

6.2 ACCUSATION OF SORCERY

In this letter, we encounter Paul in what may seem to us as a very extreme position. Paul accuses those who have been preaching against his teachings in Corinth of being "false apostles, deceitful workers, who masquerade as apostles of Christ. And no wonder, for even

---

[47] Chris Cuddy and Mark Hart, *Sword of the Spirit: A Beginner's Guide to St. Paul* (Mesa, AZ: Life Teen Inc., 2008).

Satan masquerades as an angel of light. So it is not strange that his ministers also masquerade as ministers of righteousness" (2 Cor. 11:13–15). This amounted to an accusation of sorcery. Why such a personal attack in such strong language?

In our culture, when we are confronted by people who promote something contrary to our position, we are expected to try to identify how their teachings are in error and to offer correction. We believe, in our culture's symbolic universe, that this is the appropriate response to opposition. But Paul and his listeners saw their opponents as "demons" who created disorder, or unholiness, in the Corinthian community. He tells the Corinthians that just "as the serpent deceived Eve by his cunning, your thoughts may be corrupted" (2 Cor. 11:3). This corruption was a grave infraction in a culture that was so heavily invested in the maintenance of proper order.

Indeed, to create disorder deliberately was ungodly conduct that had to be driven out. The order of truth was being subverted by the chaos of error, and to emulate God was to separate what did not belong together. The cosmic struggle between Good and Evil meant that there was disguise and deception everywhere. And so Paul accused his opponents of sorcery, which was understood as seeking advantage over others through the assistance of evil spirits, since their teachings were a disordering, polluting influence in the community.

Appropriate conduct is largely judged by the culture in which one lives. While today we would see the teachings of Paul's opponents as heresy needing correction, for Paul, words were responded to with words, albeit harsh, and weapons were responded to with weapons — and the two were never mixed. For in a community-centered culture where "you are who others say you are," words were as devastating as weapons.

6.3 The Workings of Grace

Perhaps the motive for assembling the letter fragments that make up "Second Corinthians" into one letter was that each featured Paul addressing the subject of grace—something very misunderstood in his time and for many centuries after. Gentiles were generally unfamiliar with the whole concept of grace, but Jews had long thought that "grace" (favor) was their reward from God for living virtuous lives.

Paul appears to have been one of the first to describe grace not as a favor but as a freely-given gift from God, a gift that empowered one to accomplish what he or she would otherwise be unable to do on his or her own, or to persevere under great hardship. The Corinthians needed to be reminded of this empowerment, so Paul related to them his own experience with grace:

> That I might not become too elated, a thorn in the flesh was given to me, an angel of Satan, to beat me, to keep me from being too elated. Three times I begged the Lord about this, that it might leave me, but he said to me, "*My grace is sufficient for you, for power is made perfect in weakness.*" I will rather boast most gladly of my weaknesses, in order that the power of Christ may dwell with me. (2 Cor. 12:7–9)

Through the workings of His grace, God helps us to overcome every human weakness and trial so long as we have faith in His mercy. Almighty God *can and does* give grace to mankind in answer to our internal aspirations and prayers without the use of any external sign or ceremony. This will always be possible because we, who are made in the image of God, share a spiritual nature with God, and so God is not restricted to visible symbols in dealing with mankind.

But it is known that God has also instituted certain visible rites or ceremonies as the means by which graces are to be conferred. In order to obtain those graces, it is necessary for mankind to make use of the divinely appointed means known as "sacraments" (visible, outward signs of interior, invisible grace). In all the stages and all the important moments of Christian life, we are to rely on the sacraments as the primary sources of grace, because they were instituted by Christ for that purpose (see *CCC* 1210). The "Church," that organizational unit of those with common beliefs and their teachings and hierarchy, is the treasury of the sacraments — the font from which we all receive "grace upon grace" (John 1:16, RSVCE) — and this universal Church has its origin in Christ, not in Paul's teachings.

Consequently, the sacraments are necessary because they are the supernatural means appointed for obtaining sacramental graces (see *CCC* 1129). Of particular importance is the sacrament of Eucharist, for Jesus Himself said: "Amen, amen, I say to you, unless you eat the flesh of the Son of Man and drink his blood, you do not have life within you. Whoever eats my flesh and drinks my blood has eternal life" (John 6:53–54).

It is through the understanding of grace that we are led to the understanding of the role of the Church and the necessity of the sacraments. For many centuries, there was no questioning of the necessity of the sacraments. It was not until the Reformation, when the role of the Church was challenged, that the subject of the necessity of the sacraments became an issue.

6.4 SOME OTHER INSIGHTS

When we take into account the worldview of the people Paul was writing to, we begin to make sense out of some matters that previously seemed quite odd, such as his accusation of sorcery. While we may have been trained to address only theological matters in Paul's letters, and sociological matters may seem irrelevant in our times, we can now see that the benefit of keeping in mind the worldview of Paul's time is that we not only gain an understanding of what we thought were quite odd passages, but we also receive deeper insights into many of the theology-centered passages that we now find we didn't quite fully understand before.

SEVEN

✠ ✠ ✠

THE LETTER TO THE ROMANS

7.1 SOME BACKGROUND

The existence of a Christian community in Rome predates Paul's letter by quite a few years. It is not known how or when the Christian community began there, but the Roman historian Suetonius mentions an edict of the Emperor Claudius in 49 AD that ordered the expulsion of all Jews from Rome because of their behaviors on behalf of a certain "Chrestus"; this exile possibly involved a dispute in the Jewish community over Jesus as the Christ (Messiah).

Paul had planned to bring the message of Christ to the westernmost edges of the ancient world, what is now known as Spain. He planned to pass through Rome on the way, so this letter was a way of introducing himself to the people there. Rome was the only large city where Gentile Christians outnumbered Jewish Christians. Those Jews who were in Rome were several generations removed from their homeland and Jerusalem.

Paul's Letter to the Romans, written while in prison in Caesarea about 58 AD, is a powerful exposition of the doctrine of the supremacy of Christ and of faith in Christ as the source of salvation. It is also an implicit plea to the Christians of Rome, and to all Christians, to hold fast to that faith.

The principal divisions of this letter are:

+ Address (1:1–15)
+ Humanity Lost without the Gospel (1:16–3:20)
+ Justification through Faith in Christ (3:21–5:21)
+ Justification and the Christian Life (6:1–8:39)
+ Jews and Gentiles in God's Plan (9:1–11:36)
+ The Duties of Christians (12:1–15:13)
+ Conclusion (15:14–16:27)

7.2 SIN AND ITS CONSEQUENCES

By the time Paul wrote this letter, the definition of sin was evolving rapidly. For many centuries, Satan (also known as the devil) was seen as the "accuser of the people before God." That is, Satan was an adversary of God's people, not an adversary of God. However, in the first century, Christians began to see Satan and the Evil One as being one and the same being. In time, the personified being Sin was also seen as being the Evil One, *the* adversary of God.

The concept of a personified being—whether he was known as the Evil One or Satan or the devil or Sin—having power over them and rivaling God gave the first-century people an "acceptable" reason for their sinfulness. They saw themselves, essentially, as hapless victims in the cosmic struggle between God and His adversary (no matter his name), and so they were not personally responsible for their sins. If this were indeed the case, however, Jesus' salvific act would have little meaning.

When Paul wrote to the Romans, "Christ, raised from the dead, dies no more ... he died to sin once and for all" (Rom. 6:9–10), Paul was referring to Jesus dying to the realm of Sin (the personified force). For it is only through physical death that one is separated from the realm of Sin. Paul was convinced that in the absence of Christ's grace, it was impossible for humans to consistently avoid breaking one of God's rules.

So in order for Paul to convey the consequences of sin, and therefore the whole meaning of Christ's Passion, he had to move his listeners from a victim's mindset to a responsible sinner's mindset. Paul therefore starts this letter with the premise that his listeners see the Evil One as having influence over humans but not having full power over them. Mankind wants to decide on their own what they will do, without any consequences—in short, man seeks to be God—but that desire to "be God" is precisely what the tempter played on in the Garden of Eden: "You certainly will not die! God knows well that when you eat of it your eyes will be opened and you will be like gods, who know good and evil" (Gen. 3:4–5). Paul does not deny that the Evil One can tempt or mislead us, but he puts the ownership of sin back on the listener: we have the real power to choose whether or not to sin.

The greatest consequence of Adam and Eve's "original" sin was the loss of mankind's access to eternal life: that is, we now had to suffer both physical and spiritual death.[48] But at the very moment when mankind had condemned God and put Him to death, the effects of spiritual death were overcome, and, through God's greatest act of kindness, mankind's access to eternal life was restored. Theologians today identify this concept in Romans as the "Ultimate Gift of Love" explanation of Jesus' redemptive act of "becoming obedient to death, even death on a cross" (Phil. 2:8).[49]

---

[48] It is interesting to note that Paul speaks of the first sin as *Adam's* sin, not Eve's: "sin came into the world through one man and death through sin" (Rom. 5:12, RSVCE). But "we were reconciled to God through the death of his Son" (Rom. 5:10). First-century Middle Easterners would have believed that it was the duty of the man to protect what had been placed in his care, which included "the woman" (later named Eve). So to Paul's listeners, it was "Adam's sin."

[49] Compare this to the "Vicarious Satisfaction" explanation in Galatians 4:4–6 to see how Paul's understanding evolved through the influence of the Holy Spirit.

Understanding the gift of eternal life is central to the "Ultimate Gift of Love" explanation of Jesus' redemptive act. As Paul put it, "the gift of God is eternal life in Christ Jesus our Lord" (Rom. 6:23). What Jesus did for mankind revealed what had to be done; this, in turn, revealed what had been undone by Adam and Eve. Before Christ, Jews did not recognize that mankind had lost access to eternal life through Adam and Eve, as they could not even imagine the idea of sharing eternal life with God.

The argument that Jesus ransomed us from our sins (see the "Vicarious Satisfaction" explanation in Galatians 4:4-6) conformed more to contemporary ideas about the nature of god(s), and so many Christians found Paul's "Ultimate Gift of Love" explanation difficult to accept. During the 1960s and 1970s, some revisionists even argued that Paul "invented much of Christianity," particularly the belief in the gift of eternal life.[50] However, Jesus Himself spoke of the gift of eternal life nearly twenty years *before* Paul's letters, Jesus' teachings would have been well known through the oral tradition long before the Gospels were written.

Paul taught that both Christ's Passion *and* His Resurrection were required to overcome the consequence of sin: spiritual and physical death. Paul believed that the redemptive act had to be completely fulfilled by Christ rising from the dead and overcoming the effects of physical death so that we, too, might be raised from the dead. And so there is no division between the "theology of the Cross" and the "theology of Resurrection," a distinction that was popular in the 1960s and 1970s: both events are necessary for our hope and salvation.

7.3 RIGHTEOUSNESS AND JUSTIFICATION

Paul understood the word "righteousness" (in Greek, *dikaiosyne*) differently than other Scripture writers. Other authors generally

---

[50] Wills, *What Paul Meant.*

understood "righteousness" in the same terms as the Hebrew word *tzedakah*, which meant to hold justice and mercy in right balance, as God does. However, Paul used "righteousness" to mean one's *self* being in right balance with God:

> Indeed, if Abraham was justified on the basis of his works, he has reason to boast; but this was not so in the sight of God. For what does the scripture say? "Abraham believed God, and it was credited to him as righteousness." (Rom. 4:2–3)

Paul also used the Greek word *dikaioma* (which is usually translated as "justification") to mean one's self being in right balance with God (see Rom. 4:25). This use of two different terms to mean essentially the same thing has confused many listeners and readers who are not versed in "Paul-speak," but any distinction between these terms seems inconsequential (remember that in Galatians 3:11, *dikaiosyne* is translated into English as both "righteousness" and as "justification"). It's possible that "righteousness" appealed more to Jews and "justification" appealed more to Gentiles; we just don't know. People today think of "righteousness" as an ongoing state in life and being "justified" (or having "justification") as happening as a single event, but this is clearly not the understanding Paul intended.

7.4 BAPTISM AND "NEW CREATION"

All religions that proclaim "salvation" have to deal with the fact that we all die. Christianity proclaims salvation from both sin and death: through the Passion and death of Jesus, we are saved not from physical death in this life but from spiritual death (that is, being deprived of eternal life with God). Paul called this liberation from the eternal effects of sin the "newness of life":

Are you unaware that we who were baptized into Christ Jesus were baptized into his death? We were indeed buried with him through baptism into death, so that, just as Christ was raised from the dead by the glory of the Father, we too might live in *newness of life*. (Rom. 6:3–4)

In the ancient world, people were baptized by full emersion in water; then they were raised up from the water. To this day, adults may be baptized in this way. This experience acts out dying to one's former self, who had no access to eternal life with God because of Original Sin, and rising to new life as a "new creation" who now has access to eternal life with God: "Whoever is in Christ is a *new creation*: the old things have passed away; behold, new things have come" (2 Cor. 5:17).

By way of this dying and rising, we are in union with Christ's dying and rising and therefore will be resurrected just as He was: "For if we have grown into union with him through a death like his, we shall also be united with him in the resurrection" (Rom. 6:5).

It's unfortunate that the practice of pouring water over the head of one being baptized gives the impression that the person is simply being "washed" of Original Sin. Paul clearly understood that Baptism does not wash; it acts out dying and rising. Our former self, who we "die to," was bound by the gravest consequence of Original Sin, being deprived of access to eternal life with God, but then we rise again to new life in Christ.

THE LETTER TO THE ROMANS

Baptism, however, does not liberate us from the lesser consequence of Original Sin: physical death; Christ's salvific act radically altered the meaning of physical death, but it did not abolish it.[51]

7.5 CHRIST OUR SAVIOR

Paul used the Koine Greek word *soter*, which is usually translated as "Savior," rather than *lytrotes*, which is usually translated as "Redeemer" (see Rom. 1:16; 11:11; 13:11), in order to distance his listeners from their current understanding of redemption.

In those days, redemption referred to buying freedom for debt-slaves. As has been mentioned, it is estimated that, in the first century AD, every one in five persons in the Roman Empire was an indentured servant, or debt-slave.[52] To Paul, we were saved by Christ out of profound love, not as a result of ransom (redemption). This was, to Paul, the "new covenant" (or promise) the prophets had spoken of in Jeremiah 31:31, Ezekiel 18:31, and Isaiah 65:17. "For the law of the spirit of life in Christ Jesus freed you from the law of sin and death" (Rom. 8:2).

In Paul's time, the terms "redemption" and "ransom" were used exclusively in relation to slaves and hostages. Christ did indeed set mankind free from the "slavery" of sin, but to refer to Him in the first century as Redeemer invited questions like, "Who exacted the ransom?" and, "To whom was the ransom paid?" These and similar questions often result in God the Father being portrayed as an adversary of mankind. In moving away from that line of thinking, Paul referred to Jesus as "Savior" and His work as "salvation" (Romans 1:16; 11:11; 13:11) or "reconciliation" (Romans 5:10-11; 11:15). In Paul's

---

[51] Fr. Raymond E. Brown, "The Pauline Letters," in *An Introduction to the New Testament* (New Haven, CT: Yale University Press, 1997).

[52] "Slavery in the Roman World."

85

understanding, the death of Christ on the cross is for us a grace (*charis*) from God. In His mercy, God gave us this grace while we could not earn it; while we had no means to merit it; while we had no reason to expect it. Jesus' saving act was unilateral and totally gratuitous. He is truly our Savior. In this, mankind's reconciliation with God is permanent and there is no possibility of a *quid pro quo* on our part. To Paul, this is the "new covenant." Nothing short of this could totally set mankind free from the "slavery" of sin (see Romans 8:2).

7.6 Trichotomy of Man

Today, we are accustomed to thinking of man as consisting of body and soul. We see physical death as the separation of the soul from the body. The body decays, but the soul goes on to God. The ancient Jewish people, however, believed that man consisted of mind (Greek: *nous*) and heart (Greek: *kardia*). Upon death, the God-given life-breath (Greek: *pneuma*) left, the *kardia* decayed, and the *nous* went to *Sheol* (Greek: *Hades*, English: "underworld"), where the afterlife was lived. To a Jew, the breath was not part of the person, it was what God "breathed" into the person to give him or her life: "The Lord God formed the man out of the dust of the ground and blew into his nostrils the breath of life, and the man became a living being" (Gen. 2:7). Jews believed that the breath was what turned man from a lifeless collection of matter into a living creature.[53]

[53] As far as the afterlife was concerned, Jews believed that whether or not one was among those at the Banquet of Abraham or in Sheol depended on his or her actions during life. There was no concept of Hell prior to Jesus' teachings about the Final Judgment; to Jews, reward and punishment were meted out during earthly life. Paul, however, believed that the "afterlife" was the resurrection from the dead to eternal life, which would happen at the *Parousia*. Paul expected the *Parousia* to be "any day now," so there was no thought given, in those days, to what happened between the time of one's death and the *Parousia*.

In the Greco-Roman world, the *soma* (body), *psyche* (soul) and *pneuma* (spirit) made up the human person, whose physical structure was *sarx*, usually translated as "flesh." This division into three parts is known as trichotomy. It is clear that the Gentile view of what constituted the human person and the Jewish view of the human person were quite different, and as we read Scripture, we need to discern which view is being referred to in the text. It's sometimes confusing. For example, when Luke, who was a Gentile, said that Jesus "breathed his last" (Luke 23:46), he was referring to the Jewish view of death. But when Matthew, who was a Jew, wrote that Jesus "gave up his spirit" (Matt. 27:50), he was referring to the Greco-Roman view of death.

Paul regularly used the Greco-Roman view in his letters:

✠ "May your spirit [*pneuma*] and soul [*psyche*] and body [*soma*] be kept sound and blameless." (1 Thess. 5:23, RSVCE)

✠ "So that no human being [*sarx*] might boast before God." (1 Cor. 1:29)

✠ "Brothers, we are not debtors to the flesh [*sarx*], to live according to the flesh [*sarx*]. For if you live according to the flesh [*sarx*], you will die, but if by the spirit [*pneuma*] you put to death the deeds of the body [*soma*], you will live." (Rom. 8:12–13)

In that last passage from Romans, Paul contrasted spirit (*pneuma*) with body (*soma*). Here he was using *pneuma* to mean that which is of God, *soma* to mean that which is not of God, and *sarx* to mean our fallen human nature. In this context, *soma* is always in opposition to *pneuma*. Unfortunately, misunderstanding this passage gave rise to the interpretation that Paul taught that the body, and things of the body, are always evil.

7.7 THE UNFAIRNESS OF LIFE

In Paul's time, Jews found it very hard to accept his teaching that the gift of our salvation is entirely unmerited. (see Romans 3:20-24; 5:1-2). This stemmed largely from their history. After the Babylonian Captivity, Israel became a protectorate of Persia, which exposed them to the religion known as Zoroastrianism. A principle taught by Zoroaster was that the unfairness of life could be eliminated by everyone getting the same benefit for their efforts. In time, Jews adopted a version of this: "we must earn all that we receive in life." Many people to this day want to think that we "earn" our salvation by being good, commandment-observing people.

7.8 FAITH AND BELIEF

The Koine Greek word *pistis* is usually translated as "faith," and *elpis* is usually translated as "hope." However, the Hebrew word *emuna* often meant both faith and hope. So to a Jew, faith always involved some element of hope; but, to Gentiles faith was separate and distinct from hope.

The Koine Greek verb *pisteuein* is usually translated into English as "believe." *Pisteuein* was the Greek word used throughout the Septuagint text of the Hebrew Bible for the Hebrew word *amn*, which means "to abide by as true," and from which we get the word "amen." With this in mind, when Paul wrote, "If you confess with your mouth that Jesus is Lord and believe (*pisteusēs*) in your heart that God raised him from the dead, you will be saved" (Rom. 10:9).

We understand that to have faith in the resurrection of the dead is more than an intellectual acquiescence; it is a lived-out realization of what the "good news" means. In Paul's view, having faith in the crucified Christ requires self-emptying, a daily "crucifixion" of self out of love for others. This is how the freely given gift of our salvation is accepted. As Paul put it, "God proves his love for us in that while we were still sinners Christ died for us" (Rom. 5:8).

7.9 Some Other Insights

Many readers find Paul's letter to the Romans both fascinating and frustrating. Scott Hahn, in his commentary on Romans, observed that Romans is a demanding read;[54] this seems to have been evident even in apostolic times. As Peter wrote, "there are some things hard to understand" in Paul's letters (see 2 Pet. 3:16).

One source of difficulty for modern readers of this letter was the dominance of duality in the worldview of Paul's first listeners. As we now understand, they, and Paul, were all raised in a culture that heavily relied on order. Paul held firm to that focus. Their worldview was very authoritarian and hierarchical: everything and everyone had their "proper place."

And Paul was also a "Jew's Jew," knowing well the Jewish model of order: what was "pure" vs. what was "polluted." In this worldview, your personal conduct was less important than which side of the cosmic struggle you were on. For them, it was the *hagioi* (usually translated as "saints") against the *adikoi* (usually translated as "unjust"). This dualistic view is quite prominent in Paul's letter to the Romans. To our ears, such thinking may seem harsh, almost "non-Christian." But we need to remember that Paul's first audience saw the world in very "black and white" terms; there were no shades of grey.

Some examples of duality in the Letter to the Romans:

---

[54] Scott Hahn, *Catholic Commentary on Sacred Scripture: Romans* (Grand Rapids, MI: Baker Academic, 2017).

✠ Dualistic Views of People
- those called vs. those not called (see Rom. 1:6–7; 8:28)
- those loved vs. those not loved (see Rom. 9:13)
- those beloved vs. those not beloved (see Rom. 9:25)
- those destined vs. those not destined (see Rom. 8:29)
- my people vs. not my people (see Rom. 9:26)
- the passionate vs. the discerning (see Rom. 10:2)

✠ Dualistic Views of Time
- then vs. now (see Rom. 6:17–22)
- reign of sin vs. reign of Christ (see Rom. 5:12–21)
- under the law vs. not under the law (see Rom. 7:6)
- before circumcision vs. after (see Rom. 4:10)
- mystery hidden vs. revealed (see Rom. 16:25–26)

This dualistic view of time is important for us to keep in mind as we reflect on Paul's description of sin and death. Paul wrote: "Christ, raised from the dead, dies no more ... he died to sin once and for all" (Rom. 6:9–10). To Paul, the salvific act of Christ was *the* defining time mark in history that defined the "before" from the "after" for all mankind. To Paul, the role of physical death was to separate man from the reign of Sin (the personified being). Humans died once and then were permanently separated from Sin. Spiritual death, however, was the loss of access to eternal life with God. Christ overcame spiritual death by dying on the Cross, and He overcame physical death by rising from the dead. When Paul wrote "death no longer has power over him" (Rom. 6:9b), he was referring to both consequences of death. For what matters most is the life of our eternal being, not the life of our earthbound bodies (see Rom. 6:4).

This dualistic view also served to reinforce the "boundary" between those who were "living in Christ" and those who were not. Rituals that reinforced boundaries were a big part of first-century life. In fact, many of Jesus' parables describe the Final Judgment as a separation ritual—God's ultimate expression of order, reinforcing the eternal boundary between Good and Evil. In several of Jesus' parables, He told of sheep separated from goats; wise virgins from foolish ones; profitable servants from unprofitable ones; wheat from chaff; good fish from bad fish; those without a wedding garment from those who have, and so on. The Final Judgment, then, was seen as the final act of separation—what does not belong together will be permanently separated.

Nevertheless, in affirming the full status of Gentiles (see Rom. 1:16; 2:9; 10:12), the Jews had to accept some "divine disorder." Jews saw themselves as heirs of the covenant with Abraham; they were the "chosen people," and Gentiles were not. Yet Paul wrote: "There is no partiality with God" (Rom. 2:11). While Jews believed that God can, and does, act in "disorderly" ways (see Rom. 11:33–34), Paul and his audience seemed to have struggled a bit with this "disorder." In more than one place in this letter, Paul used the phrase: "Jew first and then Greek" (Rom. 1:16; 2:9; 2:10) implying God privileging the Jews. He also urged tolerance for those who observed different ordering of foods (see Rom. 14:1–4) and different ordering of actions (see Rom. 14:5–7). Much of this letter therefore sought to bridge the worldview that most of Paul's listeners grew up with the new, Christian worldview.

EIGHT

✠ ✠ ✠

THE LETTER TO THE PHILIPPIANS

8.1 SOME BACKGROUND

Philippi, in northeastern Greece, was a city of great importance in the Roman province of Macedonia. It was located on the trade route known as the Via Egnatia, which ran from the Adriatic Sea coast to Byzantium (later known as Constantinople). Philippi was also in the midst of rich agricultural plains near the gold deposits of Mount Pangaeus. Paul, according to Acts (see Acts 16:9–40), established at Philippi the first Christian community in Europe. He came to Philippi on his second missionary journey, probably in 49 or 50 AD, accompanied by Silas, Timothy, and Luke. Paul and Silas were forced out of Philippi, so they went on to Thessalonica.

Later, when Paul was in prison in Caesarea, the Philippians sent a deacon named Epaphroditus to visit Paul with news that there were false teachers who threatened to impose on the Philippians the burdens of the Mosaic law, including circumcision. Paul's first letter, written about 59 AD, responded to those issues and was hand-carried by Epaphroditus to Philippi. It was soon followed by what appears to be two other letters. The three letters have been combined into what we know today as Paul's Letter to the Philippians.

The three letters are:

1. an exhortation letter explaining the circumstances of his imprisonment and urging unity and solidarity within the Church (1:1–3:1; 4:4–7, 21–23)
2. a brief letter of thanksgiving (4:10–20)
3. a polemical letter warning against the threat of opponents (3:2–4:3; 4:8–9)

The principal divisions of the resulting document are:

✠ Address (1:1–11)
✠ Progress of the Gospel (1:12–26)
✠ Instructions for the Community (1:27–2:18)
✠ Travel Plans of Paul and His Assistants (2:19–3:1)
✠ Righteousness and the Goal in Christ (3:2–21)
✠ Instructions for the Community (4:1–9)
✠ Gratitude for the Philippians' Generosity (4:10–20)
✠ Farewell (4:21–23)

8.2 THE ROLE OF HYMNS IN THE EARLY CHURCH

When Pliny the Younger investigated Christians for Emperor Trajan in the year 112 AD, he concluded that Christian beliefs and rituals were "depraved, excessive superstition." However, in his description of Christian practices, Pliny mentions that even these earliest Christians joined together and sang hymns. It was through hymns that the faith was taught and regularly affirmed, a technique known in Greek as *paraenesis*. Philippians 2:6–11 is one such hymn that Paul incorporated into his letter. Paul's followers continued that practice in 1 Timothy 2:5–6 and, possibly, in Colossians 1:15–20.

[Christ], though he was in the form of God,
did not regard equality with God
something to be grasped.
Rather, he emptied himself,
taking the form of a slave,
coming in human likeness;
and found human in appearance,
he humbled himself,
becoming obedient to death,
even death on a cross.
Because of this, God greatly exalted him,
and bestowed on him the name
that is above every name,
that at the name of Jesus
every knee should bend,
of those in heaven and on earth and under the earth,
and every tongue confess that
Jesus Christ is Lord,
to the glory of God the Father.

(Philippians 2:6–11)

It's likely that the Philippians were already familiar with the words of this hymn or confession of faith. Paul includes it in his letter simply to reinforce not only the centrality of the Philippians' faith in Christ but also their identity in Christ.

8.3 BEING "INCOMPLETE"

Paul also had very vocal opponents in Philippi. Throughout all of Paul's ministry, Christianity was still part of Judaism. These false teachers were trying to impose on the Philippian converts the burdens of Mosaic law, including circumcision. And so Paul wrote:

"Beware of the dogs! Beware of the evil-workers! Beware of the mutilation!" (Phil. 3:2). In the Middle East, dogs were considered the lowest form of animal life, and to be an evil-worker was to be the lowest form of human life. Paul was meeting opposition with harsh words—a culturally appropriate response.

But Paul went one step further. He said to the Philippians, "Beware of the mutilation!" In Judaism, circumcision (or *brit milah*) was normally performed on male infants on the eighth day after birth and on male adults when they converted to Judaism (see Gen. 17:10–13). This tradition was in keeping with the Abrahamic covenant with God, and it marked the Jews as "a chosen race" (1 Pet. 2:9). By calling circumcision "the mutilation," Paul was basically saying to his audience that circumcision only had meaning when it was done for the right reason—to mark one as an heir in the Abrahamic covenant. When done for the wrong reason, it amounted to bodily mutilation. A mutilated body was not "holy" because it was "incomplete." And as noted earlier, in their culture's symbolic universe, a body that was not complete or that was deformed in some way was not "holy" because it did not exhibit proper order.

Here, Paul chose to attack the worldview of the false teachers instead of offering theological reasons against circumcision, reasons with which Gentile converts would have little connection. Paul did indeed believe that there was a good theological reason for a Jew to be circumcised—Jews were heirs of the Abrahamic covenant! And we know that Paul supported the idea of Jews being circumcised because of the story of Timothy's circumcision in Acts 16:1–3. Timothy was the son of a Jewish woman, but his father was a Greek, and Timothy was not circumcised. This made him an "incomplete" Jew, so Paul circumcised Timothy.

There was, however, good theological reason for converts not to be circumcised. As Paul stated in his letter to the Romans:

> For those who are led by the Spirit of God ...
> you received a spirit of adoption, through
> which we cry, "Abba, Father!" The Spirit itself
> bears witness with our spirit that we are chil-
> dren of God, and if children, then heirs, heirs of
> God and joint heirs with Christ, if only we suf-
> fer with him so that we may also be glorified
> with him. (Rom. 8:14–17)

All Christians were joint heirs with Christ: Jews and Gentiles. So
there was nothing gained by a Gentile being circumcised—indeed,
in their worldview, there was loss.

8.4 EVOLVING CHRISTOLOGY

Christology (i.e., how Christ is described) evolved over time from
"Jesus of Nazareth," to "Risen Lord," to the pre-existing "Son of
God," to the "Second Person of the Trinity." Prior to the Resurrec-
tion, no Jew would have referred to Jesus as *kyros* (Lord), for no
Jew would have addressed another person with the title reserved
for God alone. Paul was in the midst of this evolving Christology.
At the time of his writing to the Philippians, Paul's Christology
was at the "son of God" stage, and he referred to Christ as *kyros*
(Lord) and felt that all Christ was and did was for the "glory of
God the Father" (Phil. 2:11).[55]

Paul reflected on what Jesus did for us and concluded, just as
Jesus had said, that it was "necessary that the Messiah should suffer
these things and enter into his glory" (Luke 24:26). As we reflected
on earlier, at the very moment when mankind had condemned God

---

[55] The concept of God as a Trinity was not articulated until well into the
late second century AD.

and put Him to death, mankind's access to eternal life was restored, and this gift of love overcame the effect of spiritual death.

8.5 SOME OTHER INSIGHTS

Paul's strong desire for order and clear roles in the Church, as well as his acute sense of a larger world in which "proper" boundaries were threatened, manifested itself in this letter as well. An example of this desire for order can be found in one of the most beloved expressions of counsel offered by Paul:

> Do everything without grumbling or question-
> ing, that you may be blameless [amemptoi] and
> innocent [akeraioi], children of God without
> blemish in the midst of a crooked and perverse
> generation, among whom you shine like lights in
> the world. (Phil. 2:14–15)

The Koine Greek word *amemptoi* more accurately meant "being without defect," and the word *akeraioi* meant "not being mingled or mixed." Both words had more of an orderliness connotation than a morality connotation. This is not to say that morality was unimportant, but we must remember that to Paul's first audience, orderliness imitated God. Today, when orderliness is normally not connected with godliness, these words receive a more morality-centered translation.

We also see Paul's focus on order in the following verse: "My eager expectation and hope is that I shall not be put to shame in any way, but that with all boldness, now as always, Christ will be magnified in my *body*, whether by life or by death" (Phil. 1:20). While this is an often-quoted verse, many people puzzle over why Christ will be magnified in Paul's "body" and not in his faith or in his actions.

Recall from section 1.5 that to first century people, control over the physical body both encouraged and reflected proper order. The more bodily behaviors were controlled, the more one reflected the orderliness of God.

This attention to proper order is also manifested in Paul's cautions to the Philippians about false teachers. Paul did not address or refute "what" they were teaching, but he did make it clear that these false teachers were transgressing the orderly boundaries of the church community by teaching something different from what Paul had taught (see Phil. 1:15–18, 3:2–3).

What constitutes "proper order" of course depends on a frame of reference. The world in which Paul and his listeners were socialized was much different than the world in which we were socialized. In the times when this letter was written, it was thought that it was God's blessings that enabled mankind to live. God created order that man's affairs may prosper. God's primary act of blessing, therefore, was creation. So, the preservation of order, particularly the orderly boundaries of the church community, was preservation of the work of God.

NINE

✠ ✠ ✠

PAUL'S "OTHER LETTERS"

We have come to the end of what is referred to as the undisputed Pauline letters. After Paul's release from prison in Caesarea, he returned to Corinth for a collection to benefit the "saints in Jerusalem." He intended to visit Rome on his way to Spain, but there is no evidence that Paul ever reached Spain. Upon arriving in Jerusalem, he was soon arrested and imprisoned. He was taken to Rome in chains, and he demanded a trial by Caesar, since he was a Roman citizen. He was placed under house arrest in Rome in 61 AD, but he was not martyred until 67 AD. And so we enter a period when it is not clear whether certain letters, Paul's "other letters," were written by Paul or by others on his behalf.

9.1 AUTHOR VS. WRITER

As noted earlier in section 1.6, there are six letters attributed to Paul that many scholars contend were not written by Paul. These are broken into two categories: Paul's "Pastoral Letters," Titus, 1 Timothy, and 2 Timothy; and the "Pseudo-Pauline Letters," Colossians, Ephesians, and 2 Thessalonians.

In ancient times, the "author" of a work was the authority behind it, not necessarily the "writer" of the work. Indeed, the "author" might have lived years, even centuries, before the "writer." In addition, the "writer" often did not actually write the work but rather dictated it to a *grammateus*, or "scribe." Today, we would call someone who wrote on behalf of another, or wrote using the authority of another, a "ghost-writer." No such distinctions were made in the ancient world.

While this practice was well-known in the ancient world, it was not until the late 1700s that Ferdinand Christian Baur, founder of the Tübingen School of Theology, became the first in the Western world to point out the prevalence of this practice in biblical times.[56] At first, this caused alarm. In the past, there had been many forged Church documents in circulation; and Baur's statement suddenly cast all scriptural texts as suspect, perhaps fraudulent.

In time, however, scholars came to realize that the practice was not an attempt to deceive but was instead just "the way things were done" in the ancient world. It was often the case that a member, or members, of the author's "school of disciples" wrote in the author's name in a manner similar to how the author would have written in the situation addressed. This practice was not an attempt to deceive the readers or listeners; rather, a disciple was simply assuming the great author's mantle and continuing his master's work in the world.[57]

True as this all may be, scholars were left with a very practical problem. If the "writer" was not the "author," how well did the text reflect the author's thinking and teachings, and how much did it reflect changes in thinking or world events that followed the author's death? This leads to a larger consideration in Scripture interpretation. In Scripture, we are reading the inspired word of

---

[56] Fr. Raymond E. Brown, "Pseudonymity and the Deutero-Pauline Writings," in *An Introduction to the New Testament* (New Haven, CT: Yale University Press, 1997).

[57] Ibid.

God. Therefore, knowing the actual writer is of little importance. Knowing the approximate timing of the actual writing, however, helps us place the text in its cultural context, for we are ultimately relying on the Holy Spirit, not the writer, to lead us.

9.2 BEGINNING OF THE END TIMES

In the final years of Paul's life, and for decades thereafter, drastic changes took place in the Eastern Mediterranean world that many Christians interpreted as the "beginning of the end times."

From 54–68 AD, the Roman Empire was ruled by Emperor Nero, whose extravagant, empire-wide program of public and private works was funded by a substantial rise in taxes that was much resented by the people. Nero was an adopted heir of Emperor Claudius, his great-uncle, and he succeeded Claudius when he was not even seventeen years old. Nero's mother, Agrippina, dominated his early life and decisions, but Nero eventually cast her off.

Nero was impulsive, a tyrant, and quite likely mentally ill. His insanity is most evident in the way in which he treated those around him. For example, he ordered the poisoning of his step-brother Britannicus at a banquet in 55 AD. Then, in 59 AD, Nero had his mother murdered. He divorced first wife, Octavia, in order that he might marry Poppaea, the wife of his friend Otho, and he later ordered the killing of Octavia. Poppaea herself possibly died from injuries sustained after Nero kicked her while she was with child. And Nero's leading adviser, Seneca, was discharged and forced to commit suicide.

In the midst of these horrific acts of violence, in 64 AD, Rome caught on fire.[58] This fire began on July 19, in the merchant shops

[58] Tradition has it that Peter had come to Rome by 62 AD; it's not clear whether Paul was there at the time of the fire.

around Rome's chariot stadium. After six days, the fire was brought under control, but before the damage could be assessed, the fire reignited and burned for another three days. In the aftermath of the fire, two-thirds of the city of Rome had been destroyed. According to the ancient Roman historian Tacitus, Nero blamed the devastation on the Christian community in the city, initiating the empire's first persecution against the Christians. Other contemporary historians, however, wrote that it was widely rumored that Nero himself ordered the fire to be started in order to clear space for his new palace.

Following the Great Fire of Rome, we know of at least two men who were martyred under the reign of Nero: Sts. Peter and Paul. Tradition suggests that Peter was crucified (upside down, at Peter's request) in the Circus of Nero, where St. Peter's Basilica stands today, and that Paul was beheaded outside the city walls on the main thoroughfare known as the Ostian Way. Most historians place both martyrdoms around the year 67 AD.[59]

Nero grew progressively more insane and was eventually named a public enemy of the state. He ordered his private secretary to help him commit suicide on June 9, 68 AD. Nevertheless, in the minds of many Christians, the final tribulations and the cosmic struggle between Good and Evil had begun.

Then the culture's perception of the "proper order of things" was completely upended by a series of power struggles in Rome in 69 AD, which has become known as "the Year of the Four Emperors" and which finally ended with the general Vespasian as emperor of Rome.

During Vespasian's reign, his son Titus destroyed most of Jerusalem, including the Jewish Temple, in the summer of 70 AD. More than a million Jews in and around Jerusalem were killed. Few if any

---

[59] Abel M. Bibliowicz, *Jewish-Christian Relations: The First Centuries* (WA: Mascarat Publishing, 2019).

Christians were killed, as they had escaped Jerusalem beforehand, heeding Jesus' warning of the "end times" in His sermon on the Mount of Olives (see Matthew 24 and 25, Mark 13, and Luke 21), but this tragedy was still seen as the "proof-positive" that the end times had begun. People throughout the empire were struggling to make sense out of a world that was in turmoil, and in the struggle, Christians were often victimized, as their refusal to take place in public acts of pagan worship was often seen as "revolutionary" behavior.

Even within the Judeo-Christian world, tensions were rising as Jews and Christians scattered all over the Middle East. While Christians still saw themselves as Jews and had still been participating in Jewish synagogue services, Jews thought that Christians believed in two gods, the "Father" and the "Son." Therefore, they thought, because Christians had "polluted" their synagogue communities, God had punished His People with the destruction of the Temple. Christians were summarily expelled from the synagogues and thus abruptly and traumatically cut off from their ancestral roots.

Christians believed that Jesus must be returning "any day now," and His return would bring about the "proper order of things." However, there was urgent work to be done in the meantime. The traumatized Christian communities needed to restore proper order, have community unity, and be encouraged and strengthened by hearing the story of Jesus and His teachings and promises again and again. And so the formation of the Gospels as written books was begun.

Meanwhile, persecutions continued — predominantly under Roman governors in various provinces — and many Christians denied their faith when they were faced with the loss of their family, their children, and their loved ones. This denial was called "apostasy," and those who denied the faith were called "apostates." Until the Roman Empire legalized the practice of Christianity in 313 AD, the Church had to struggle with whether or not to accept repentant apostates back into her flock.

So in the latter half of the first century AD, the world in which Christians lived underwent such upheaval that Paul's "other letters" must have addressed issues and concerns that were new to Christian communities. If Paul's "other letters" were not written by Paul but near or after his death, then we should expect to see evidence of those new issues and concerns in those letters.

TEN

✠ ✠ ✠

THE LETTER TO TITUS

10.1 SOME BACKGROUND

Paul's missionary companion Titus is not mentioned in the Acts of the Apostles. We first hear of him in Paul's Letter to the Galatians, in which Paul told the Galatians that he took Titus, a Greek convert, with him to the first Church Council in Jerusalem in 49 AD (see Gal. 2:1–3). Titus was then dispatched to Corinth, where he successfully reconciled the Christian community there with Paul, its founder. Titus was mentioned a number of times in Paul's Second Letter to the Corinthians (2 Cor. 2:13; 7:6, 13–15; 8:6, 16, 23; 12:18). From this letter, we learn that Paul ministered in Crete for some time and left Titus there, upon his departure, to continue establishing churches on the island. At some point, Paul summoned Titus from Crete to join him at Nicopolis (Titus 3:12). This all had to have been during what many scholars call Paul's "second career."

Crete is an island southeast of Greece in the Mediterranean Sea. The island is about 150 miles long from east to west, and its width ranges from 35 miles at its widest point to 7.5 miles at its narrowest. The interior is very mountainous, woody, and interspersed by many fertile valleys. In the first century, the majority of the population lived in cities along the coast. There was no developed road system on the island, so most travel was by ferries. Few ventured inland.

There were about twenty cities in Crete during the time of early Roman Empire. They were extremely independent, issuing their own coins and administered by their own magistrates. The most prominent city was Gortyna, the administrative capital. The cities were so fiercely independent that they had a long history of warring with one another. As to the people of Crete, Paul quoted "one of their own poets" (Epimenides) to describe their character: "Cretans have always been liars, vicious beasts, and lazy gluttons" (Titus 1:12).

Under Emperor Tiberius (who ruled 14–37 AD), Crete was used for exiles from Rome. When Paul sent Titus to Crete, there was already a large Jewish presence there dating from at least the second century BC (see 1 Maccabees 15:15–24). We also know that the Cretans worshiped the Roman pantheon and were engaged in several religious cults: there is evidence that by the first century AD, the cult of Augustus and Roma was in Gortyna, the cult of the deified Claudius was in Knossos, and the cult of Asclepius, a god of healing, was in at least eighteen locations in Crete.

Tradition has it that Titus was martyred in 96 AD in the city of Gortyna, where he was also buried. He is venerated as a martyr, but the details of how he was martyred are unknown. This has prompted some scholars to contend that he was not martyred but instead died of natural causes in 107 AD. This theory would justify a second century date for this letter, and since it's reasonably clear that this letter preceded 1 and 2 Timothy, it would also place those letters in the second century. We do know that the only relic of Titus, his head, was removed from Crete during the Crusades and taken to Venice. It was returned to Crete in 1966.

The writing in this letter—indeed, in all of Paul's "Pastoral Letters"—utilizes Koine Greek participles, conjunctions, and adverbs that are notably different from those in the other Pauline letters. About one-quarter of the vocabulary in these letters does not appear in the undisputed Pauline letters, but it is very similar to the vocabulary in Acts and in the Gospel of Luke. This has led some scholars to conclude that Luke wrote this Pastoral Letters on Paul's behalf.

Regardless of author, the Pastoral Letters have a personal character, and they are written to two men whom Paul had appointed as bishops: Titus and Timothy. The different subject matter of the letters could account for some vocabulary differences, and from what we know of both Titus and Timothy, they were likely well-educated in Greek, which might account for the grammar differences, especially if Luke had been the actual writer.[60]

The principal divisions in this letter are:

✠ Address (1:1–4)
✠ Pastoral Charge (1:5–16)
✠ Teaching the Christian Life (2:1–3:15)

10.2 Creating Order in the Church

In the Pastoral Letters, we encounter three Koine Greek words that are either unique to the Pastoral Letters or are found in only one other place in Scripture. These words are typically translated into English words that connote proper moral conduct:

✠ *anepilémptos* ("irreproachable"): in 1 Tim. 3:2; 5:7; 6:14
✠ *katharos* ("pure"): in 1 Tim. 1:5; 3:9; Titus 1:15;
2 Tim. 1:3, 2:22

---

[60] Fr. Raymond E. Brown, "Pastoral Letter, the First to Timothy," in *An Introduction to the New Testament* (New Haven, CT: Yale University Press, 1997).

✣ *anegklétos* ("blameless"): in 1 Tim. 3:10; Titus 1:6, 7; Col. 1:22; 1 Cor. 1:8

In the original Koine Greek, however, these words connoted orderliness. Recall that the symbolic universe of that time was very intensely focused on order. Indeed, to be "holy" was to emulate God's orderliness.

The writer of this letter coaches Titus on putting in place some church structure as a way of creating order in the Christian community. The first step in creating church structure was to properly appoint, that is, to "ordain," presiders over the celebration of the Breaking of the Bread. Those presiders were called *presbyteros* ("presbyters"), today called "priests." And Titus was assigned the task of appointing these presbyters "in every town" (Titus 1:5).

10.3 A "NEW" CHALLENGE?

During most of Paul's ministry, opposition was primarily from Jews who tried to force the observance of the full Jewish law, including the rite of circumcision. There's no reference to that kind of opposition in this letter. Instead, we encounter, perhaps for the first time, the issue of false teachers who were presenting "Jewish myths" (Titus 1:14). But the letter does not make clear what those "Jewish myths" were.[61]

The writer here was referring to what came to be known in the second century as Gnosticism (from the Greek *gnosis*, "knowledge"), which had its early roots in Judaism.[62] Gnostics claimed that the principal element of salvation came from special knowledge of the

---

[61] We will see more details about these "Jewish myths" in the next chapter when we look at the First Letter to Timothy.

[62] Joseph Barber Lightfoot, *Notes on the Epistles of St. Paul* (1895; repr., London: Forgotten Books, 2018).

supreme divinity, knowledge in the form of mystical insights that only Gnostics had. In Gnosticism, there were no concepts of sin and repentance; rather, it was all about "enlightenment."[63]

Gnosticism was a significant problem for the early Church, but it was mostly prevalent well after Paul's death. However, there is some debate about whether Gnosticism could have been already influencing the early Christian communities during Paul's life. Let us look at 1 Corinthians, in which Paul made use of the Koine Greek word *sophia* (typically translated into English as "wisdom") several times. *Sophia*, however, is not wisdom as we are familiar with it today. Throughout much of the Old Testament, wisdom referred to knowledge of the order of nature. Since the ancient Jews saw God manifested in the order of nature, wisdom, then, would lead to knowledge of God. But by the first century AD, the meaning of wisdom had broadened to mean knowledge demonstrated in achieving an end.[64] To this day, many scholars have interpreted Paul's use of *sophia* in 1 Corinthians as Paul explaining that God's plan of salvation is achieved by Christ's death on the cross (see 1 Cor. 2:6–3:4). But with the controversy over the reference to Gnosticism in the Pastoral Letters, some scholars have pointed out that *sophia* could also mean the knowledge that is demonstrated in achieving the end of salvation. This idea was the central tenet of Gnosticism.

Now we can finally ask ourselves: was Paul addressing an early-stage problem with Gnosticism in Corinth? Many scholars say yes; many others say no. If yes, then the Gnosticism addressed in the Pastoral Letters is *not* a new challenge (this argument seems to be supported by 1 Corinthians 2:4, in which Paul clearly states the

---

[63] Aldo Magris, "Gnosticism from Its Origins to the Middle Ages," in *MacMillan Encyclopedia of Religion* (2005).

[64] Footnote to 1 Corinthians 1:17b in the *New American Bible, revised edition* (Washington: Confraternity of Christian Doctrine, 1970).

ineffectiveness of human wisdom for salvation). If no, then Gnosticism may well have been a new challenge, which would give some credibility to the assertion that the Pastoral Letters were written well after Paul's death. We may never know the answer for sure.

In the end, however, this debate does not change the faith lesson in Scripture: human wisdom is ineffective in achieving salvation. And we need to be aware that when people are being persecuted, as they seek reassurance that they will be alright, they often "grasp at straws." Gnosticism was one of those "straws," and the more that Jews and Christians were persecuted, the more people were drawn to Gnosticism, thinking that their "special knowledge" of the supreme divinity would save them.

10.4 THE HOUSEHOLD OF GOD

It is evident from this letter that the church in Crete was in its early stages of development. At this time, the *church* was regarded as the household of God. Paul therefore devotes considerable attention to bringing the orderliness of home life into the church community. The faithful are encouraged to use their example to draw others into the community (see Titus 2:7).

Some today might find part of the instructions in this letter a bit disturbing, particularly with regard to the role of women. For example, this letter instructed Titus that

> older women should be reverent in their behavior, not slanderers, not addicted to drink, teaching what is good, so that they may train younger women to love their husbands and children, to be self-controlled, chaste, good homemakers, under the control of their husbands, so that the word of God may not be discredited. (Titus 2:3-5)

In our times, many might find offensive the idea that a woman needs to be "trained" to love her husband and children, or that a woman not being "under the control of her husband" would discredit the word of God. But we need to recall an important point made above, that Paul was not always explicitly teaching theology in his letters. Rather, he was often addressing specific issues in the communities to whom he was writing. Therefore, we should not take this single passage in the Letter to Titus as fully expressing Paul's teaching on husband-wife relationships. We need to look further in the Pauline corpus before drawing some conclusions. For instance, addressing "husbands and wives," he says:

> Be subordinate to one another out of reverence for Christ. Wives should be subordinate to their husbands as to the Lord. For the husband is head of his wife just as Christ is head of the church, he himself the savior of the body. As the church is subordinate to Christ, so wives should be subordinate to their husbands in everything. Husbands, love your wives, even as Christ loved the church and handed himself over for her. (Eph 5:21–25)

It is evident from this text that Paul did not teach domination of one over the other but mutuality in the husband-wife relationship. We conclude then that, in Paul's teaching, the wife should serve her husband in the same spirit as that of the church's service to Christ while the husband should care for his wife with the devotion of Christ to the church.

10.5 SOME OTHER INSIGHTS

If we are to interpret this letter in the context in which it was written, we need to come to some conclusion about when it was written, for that influenced what the writer addressed and how the first listeners interpreted it. We've seen that the writer of this letter encouraged Titus to promote order in the Church community during what was likely a time of increasing disorder. If we look solely at this letter in its historical context, the writer certainly could have been Paul; in fact, there's little to say that he wasn't the writer, as there is no mention or hint of:

1. the destruction of the Temple in 70 AD,
2. the massacre of Jews in Jerusalem, or
3. the flight of many thousands of Christians and the traumatic expulsion of those Christians from the synagogues that followed the Jewish Revolt.

We conclude, then, that it was likely written prior to 70 AD, by Paul, or by someone acting on his behalf, either before or shortly after Paul's martyrdom.

ELEVEN

✠ ✠ ✠

THE FIRST LETTER TO TIMOTHY

11.1 SOME BACKGROUND

According to Luke's account in Acts, Paul first met Timothy in Lystra, probably in 50 AD. As noted earlier in section 8.3, Timothy was the son of a Jewish woman, but his father was a Greek. The believers in Lystra spoke highly of him, so Paul took him along on his missionary journey (Acts 16:1–3). When Paul was harassed by enemies from Thessalonica, Paul and his companions went to the nearby city of Beroea (Acts 17:10) but detractors from Thessalonica followed them. Paul hurriedly left for Athens, but Timothy and Silas remained behind in Beroea for a while. Later, Paul sent Timothy back to Thessalonica to strengthen that community in its trials (1 Thess 3:2).

We don't know at what point Paul ordained Timothy by the laying-on of hands, but we do know that Timothy, and another disciple named Erastus, were Paul's "helpers" during his long teaching ministry in Ephesus. Timothy acted as Paul's messenger to carry the Corinthian correspondence from Ephesus, and his name is linked with Paul's in letters to Thessalonica, Colossae, and Philippi.

Sometime following Paul's third missionary journey, Paul appointed Timothy as his representative in Ephesus to teach there for a considerable time. Since it was not mentioned in Acts of the

Apostles, this appointment could have been during what some scholars call Paul's "second career." Eusebius, the fourth-century historian and bishop of Caesarea, recorded that Timothy was the first bishop of Ephesus.

In the first century AD, Ephesus, known as the "Mother City of Asia," was the most important city in the Roman Empire outside of Rome. It had a busy seaport and was at the junction of two trade routes into the interior of Asia Minor, and it served as the center of commerce and communications for the eastern Roman Empire. Ephesus was also a distinctly religious city; their "favorite" god was the goddess Artemis (see Acts 19:35), and her temple, which was one of the largest buildings in the world at the time, was home to elaborate, women-led fertility rites. The Temple of Artemis, or Diana as the Romans called her, also served as the largest bank in the Roman Empire.[65]

Tradition holds that toward the end of their lives, the apostle John and Mary, the mother of Jesus, lived in Ephesus. A small stone house, known as The House of the Virgin Mary, still stands to this day on Bulbul Hill outside of what remains of Ephesus, and it is believed that John wrote his Gospel in Ephesus.

There was always an unsettled relationship between the Christian community and the larger population of Ephesus, as Christians were, by their very nature, upsetting the order of the pagan community. But during Roman-led persecution of Christians, following the Great Fire of Rome in 64 AD, they were in peril much of the time. During that period, Ephesus was the center of the Roman practice of *damnatio ad bestas* ("condemnation to beasts") — having condemned persons killed by wild beasts, usually lions, for the "entertainment of the masses."[66]

---

[65] Steve M. Baugh, "A Foreign World: Ephesus in the First Century," in *Women in the Church* (Wheaton, IL: Crossway Publishers, 2005).

[66] Alison Futrell, *Blood in the Arena: The Spectacle of Roman Power* (Austin, TX: University of Texas Press, 1997).

Sadly, in the year 97 AD, Timothy tried to stop a licentious procession in honor of the goddess Diana, and he was stoned to death by an angry mob. This may not have been a matter of Christian persecution but rather of a mob having been incensed over Timothy's interference in their procession.

Since Ephesus was so devoted to its pagan cult, we might wonder: why would Paul or Timothy or John go there? The answer is the same as to why Jesus went to Capernaum. Just like Ephesus, Capernaum was a "crossroads" location, and missionaries went to "crossroads" because people were always coming and going. These people were more open to new ideas than those in an established community. So missionaries braved the hostility of the local communities to reach the many who were open to listening.

The principal divisions in this letter are:

✣ Address (1:1–2)
✣ Sound Teaching (1:3–20)
✣ Problems of Discipline (2:1–4:16)
✣ Duties toward Others (5:1–6:2a)
✣ False Teaching and True Wealth (6:2b–19)
✣ Final Recommendation and Warning (6:20–21)

11.2 BEING FOR OTHERS

Similar to in the Letter to Titus, the writer of this letter counseled Timothy to promote orderliness in himself and in the clergy, even to "reprimand publicly those who do sin, so that the rest also will be afraid" (1 Tim 5:20) This very much reflects Paul's philosophy of being for others what they need most (e.g. 1 Cor 9:19-23).

In this letter, we see evidence that the world around the Christian community in Ephesus was in great disorder. They were in the "beginning of the end times"—in the midst of a great power struggle in the Roman Empire and intensified tension between Christians and Jews.

Remember that in the worldview of first-century Jews and Christians, people influenced the social order around them by maintaining order in their own behavior, and people separated themselves from those who were not orderly, as they were considered to be "unholy"). Consequently, these words of counsel to Timothy set the example of being orderly oneself and of choosing persons to lead who are orderly and to whom the community can look for guidance and example.

11.3 PROMOTE ORDER IN THE CHURCH

There are four sections in the First Letter to Timothy that are seen as controversial today, but each can be understood better in its proper context of promoting order in the community of the church in Ephesus as well as the greater Church.

First, it is clear that at the time of this letter, there was an established clergy in the Church. The writer reminded Timothy of the qualifications needed in this three-level clergy that still exists to this day:

✣ *episkopos* ("bishop") in 1 Timothy 3:1–7
✣ *presbyteros* ("presbyter," today called "priest") in 1 Timothy 5:17–19
✣ *diakonos* ("deacon") in 1 Timothy 3:8–10

In the sixteenth century, most "reformation" theologians argued that there was no established clergy in the first century; they claimed that the Pastoral Letters were written by someone other than Paul and sometime in the second century.[67] But this theory

---

[67] Donald A. Carson and Douglas Moo, *An Introduction to the New Testament* (Grand Rapids, MI: Zondervan Academic, 2005).

cannot be true, since the Pastoral Letters provided counsel to two well-known individuals, Titus and Timothy, and from the best information we have, Titus died a martyr in 96 AD, and Timothy died a martyr in 97 AD. Why would someone in the second century write letters, in the name of Paul, giving counsel to two men whom the whole Church knew very well had been martyred in the previous century?

This letter also goes on to counsel Timothy on the proper conduct of women in church:

> It is my wish, then, that in every place the men should pray, lifting up holy hands, without anger or argument. Similarly, [too,] women should adorn themselves with proper conduct, with modesty and self-control, not with braided hairstyles and gold ornaments, or pearls, or expensive clothes, but rather, as befits women who profess reverence for God, with good deeds. A woman must receive instruction silently and under complete control. (1 Tim. 2:8–11)

Some find this passage disproportionately restrictive of women. In addition, there are several "rules" for widows given in 1 Timothy 5:3–16. But we need to recall that the writer is speaking in the context of contrasting the behavior of Christian women with the licentious conduct of women in the Temple of Artemis in Ephesus.

The third controversial passage in this letter is:

> Moreover, they [deacons] should be tested first; then, if there is nothing against them, let them serve as deacons. Women, similarly, should be

dignified, not slanderers, but temperate and faithful in everything. (1 Tim. 3:10–11)

Some scholars read this as meaning that there were women deacons in Ephesus. Unfortunately, there was no female form of *diakonos* in Koine Greek.[68] So the precise meaning of this passage is inconclusive.

And there is yet another controversial passage concerning women and clergy:

Do not rebuke an *older man*, but appeal to him as a father. Treat younger men as brothers, *older women* as mothers, and younger women as sisters with complete purity. (1 Tim. 5:1–2)

The Koine Greek word that is translated as "older women" is *presbyteras*, the female form of the noun *presbyteros*. Some scholars read this as meaning that there were female priests in Ephesus. However, the formal meaning of *presbyteros* is "older man." In biblical passages, *presbyteros* was used to stand for "elder," both those who served as elders in the Jewish Sanhedrin and those who served as "presiders" in early Christian house-churches. In this passage from 1 Timothy, it is reasonably clear that the term "older women" was used in contrast to "older man" from the previous verse.

11.4 THE "NEW" CHALLENGE

The Letter to Titus touched on the new threat to Christian communities. Evidently, the issue was more acute in Ephesus, as his letter speaks about false doctrines (1 Tim. 1:3), fruitless discussions (1 Tim. 1:6), another doctrine (1 Tim. 6:3–4), and false knowledge (1 Tim. 6:20).

---

[68] Mounce, *Basics of Biblical Greek.*

But it also mentions what appears to be the new challenge, what the writer refers to as "myths,"(1 Tim 1L4) and "silly myths" (1 Tim 4:7). The letter is also not clear on what these "myths" are, but a number of scholars contend that this is early evidence in the Christian communities of what would later be known as Gnosticism.

11.5 SOME OTHER INSIGHTS

Just as we did with the letter to Titus, if we are to interpret this letter in the context in which it was written, we need to come to some conclusion on when it was written. We've seen that the writer of this letter encouraged Timothy to remain firm and promote order in his own life and in the Church community during what was likely an environment of disorder. The writer certainly could have been Paul, in fact there's little to say that it wasn't, since just as in the Letter to Titus, this letter makes no mention or hint of:

1. the destruction of the Temple in 70 AD,
2. the massacre of Jews in Jerusalem, or

the flight of many thousands of Christians into Asia Minor and the traumatic expulsion of those Christians from the synagogues that followed the Jewish Revolt. Accordingly, we conclude that it was likely written prior to 70 AD, by Paul, or by someone acting on his behalf, either before or shortly after Paul's martyrdom.

Just as they were likely experiencing, in our own times, we are also surrounded by a world of increasing disorder. The details are different, but the human effects are very similar—people grasp at any idea or movement that promises quick solutions to social injustice. It's in being steadfast, in holding to the truth, just as this letter stressed, that good shall ultimately prevail.

TWELVE

✠ ✠ ✠

THE SECOND LETTER TO TIMOTHY

12.1 SOME BACKGROUND

While the Letter to Titus and 1 Timothy provide instruction on order and church structure, 2 Timothy is silent on those subjects. Instead, 2 Timothy has the tone of a farewell address that might have been read to the entire Ephesus community. This letter recalls an earlier sorrowful parting from Timothy, commends him for his faith, and expresses a longing to see him again. Paul had committed his life to Christ, and, amidst his sufferings, he knew that God would protect what had been entrusted to him (see 2 Tim. 1:12).

The vocabulary and poetic style of this letter are closer to the "undisputed" Pauline letters than to the Koine Greek of Titus and 1 Timothy. If Paul did in fact have a "second career," then this letter indicates that he was back in prison in Rome (see 2 Tim. 1:8, 17; 4:6–8), and it anticipates his death (2 Tim. 4:7–8).[69]

The principal divisions of this letter are:

✠ Address (1:1–5)
✠ Exhortations to Timothy (1:6–2:13)

---

[69] Jerome Murphy-O'Conner, "II Timothy Contrasted with I Timothy and Titus," *Biblical Review* 98 (1991).

✠ Instructions about False Teachers (2:14–4:8)
✠ Conclusion (4:9–22)

12.2 Persecution

Bearing up under persecution appears to be the central theme of this letter. One of the strongest arguments for Paul having written this letter is found in how he reminds Timothy not to despair, for "all who want to live religiously in Christ Jesus will be persecuted" (2 Tim. 3:12). There will always be persecution of the followers of Jesus Christ, in varying degrees: Jesus Himself promised us no less (see Matt. 5:10–12; 10:16–18; Mark 10:29–30; John 15:19–20). Just hang on, Christ is with you in your suffering.

To a community in Ephesus that was likely struggling with increased persecution following the Great Fire of Rome, the writer offered a higher-level perspective.

12.3 Some Other Insights

An essential element in understanding Scripture is that it is inspired by God. If it were not, it would all be simply informative and interesting writings. In this letter, the writer reminded Timothy that "All scripture is inspired by God and is useful for teaching, for refutation, for correction, and for training in righteousness" (2 Tim. 3:16). At the time of this letter, there was no New Testament. "Scripture" here refers to the Hebrew Scripture (known by Christians as the Old Testament). In this verse, the writer is saying that their Scripture continues to be a source of learning, guidance and training in righteousness.

As for those who fail to appreciate, or accept, that Scripture is inspired by God, the writer told Timothy:

the time will come when people will not tolerate sound doctrine but, following their own desires and insatiable curiosity, will accumulate teachers and will stop listening to the truth and will be diverted to myths. (2 Tim. 4:3–4)

Here again, we come to the question, "When was this letter written?" As mentioned earlier, this letter has the tone of a farewell address that might have been read to the entire Ephesus community. It would make little sense for a disciple of Paul to write such a letter long after Paul's death. So, we place this letter right around the time of Paul's martyrdom. There is an element of linguistics that's worth noting in regard to this letter, as well as Titus and 1 Timothy. Throughout the undisputed letters of Paul, he wrote often about Jesus' awaited return using the Koine Greek word *Parousia* (which is usually translated as Coming). But, in this letter, as well as in Titus and 1 Timothy, the writer does not refer to Jesus' awaited return as *Parousia* but as *Epiphaneias* (which is usually translates as Appearance) (see Titus 2:13; 1 Tim 6:14; 2 Tim 1:10, 4:8). This gives credibility to the argument by many scholars that the Pastoral Letters were written by someone other than Paul, but on Paul's behalf, quite likely by Luke. This letter states, "Only Luke is with me" (2 Tm 4:11).

All of this is to say that our quest to identify the writer of the Pastoral Letters only has meaning to the extent that we might be better able to discern the timing of the writings and therefore understand what was going on in the world around its first listeners. The ultimate author is the Holy Spirit, and we must not to forget that.

THIRTEEN

✠ ✠ ✠

THE LETTER TO THE COLOSSIANS

13.1 SOME BACKGROUND

In order for us to better understand this letter, we first need to know a little about the city of Colossae. One of the trade routes that linked Ephesus to the Euphrates River and the Far East passed through the region known as Phrygia, which was along the Lycus River. About 110 miles east of Ephesus, on that trade route, was the tri-city area of Laodicea, Colossae, and Hieropolis. Laodicea was by far the largest of the three cities, and as a result, sometimes the people of the whole area were called Laodiceans. Colossae itself had a very prosperous trade in an expensive, purple dye called *colossinus*, which was laboriously extracted from the cyclamen flower and from which the city got its name.

There was a large Jewish population in the area who had migrated there after the Babylonian Captivity. However, by the first century AD, these Jews had been away from their homeland for many generations, and as a result, elements of their Judaism had blended with Gnostic and pagan beliefs, including the worship of lesser celestial beings or angels.[70]

[70] Frederick F. Bruce, *New Testament History* (New York: Galilee Doubleday, 1980).

In trying to discern the approximate date when the Letter to the Colossians was written, scholars have an important fixed reference point in time to work with. The Lycus River is on a geological fault known as the Denizli Basin, and the area is prone to earthquakes. There was a devastating earthquake in Colossae in 60 AD that destroyed most of the city, but the Colossians were very resilient people and rebuilt their city after this earthquake. Since this letter makes no mention of a recent earthquake or even hints at a recovery underway, the letter either preceded 60 AD or was written well after the rebuilding time—perhaps 75 AD or later. With this in mind, Paul could easily have written this letter prior to being taken as a prisoner to Rome in 61 AD.

Many scholars theorize that Paul wrote this letter while in prison in Ephesus at about the same time that he wrote the Letter to Philemon in 55 AD. Tychicus, who was entrusted to deliver this letter (Col. 4:7), could well have traveled with Onesimus when he delivered the Letter to Philemon, who was a prominent resident of Colossae.

If this letter had been written after about 75 AD, then by that time, the Christian world would have seen the destruction of the Temple, the massacre of Jews in Jerusalem, a mass exodus of Christians into Asia Minor, and the subsequent expulsion of Christians from the synagogues. But there is no hint of any of these events in this letter.

There are many scholars who contend that this letter was written by a disciple of Paul late in the first century. The Letter to the Colossians appears to precede the Letter to the Ephesians, and if Colossians was written late in the first century, then Ephesians was written even later. This theory would help explain why Ephesians was written in the form of an encyclical rather than a letter, a style that was more common in and after the late first century. (For more on this, see section 14.1).

The principal divisions in this letter are:

✠ Address (1:1–14)
✠ The Preeminence of Christ (1:15–2:3)
✠ Warnings against False Teachers (2:4–23)
✠ The Ideal Christian Life in the World (3:1–4:6)
✠ Conclusion (4:7–18)

13.2 THE LORDSHIP OF CHRIST

This letter begins with a greeting from both Paul and Timothy. Timothy may have been Paul's scribe for this letter, or Timothy could have been the writer on Paul's behalf. If the letter was written by a disciple of Paul later in the first century, then nothing would be gained by his citing the name of Timothy. By the late first century, Paul was a highly revered martyr.

The letter then continues directly into what sounds like an early Christian hymn:

> He is the image of the invisible God,
> the firstborn of all creation.
> For in him were created all things
> in heaven and on earth,
> the visible and the invisible,
> whether thrones or dominions
> or principalities or powers;
> all things were created through him and for him.
> He is before all things,
> and in him all things hold together.
> He is the head of the body, the church.
> He is the beginning, the firstborn from the dead,
> that in all things he himself might be preeminent.

For in him all the fullness was pleased to dwell,
and through him to reconcile all things for him,
making peace by the blood of his cross
[through him], whether those on earth
or those in heaven. (Col. 1:15–20)

This "hymn" is puzzling. Hymns were used in the early church to teach and regularly affirm the faith. But the Christology (how Christ is described) in this text is much more advanced than it is in the hymn found in the Letter to the Philippians. In fact, this hymn is much like the hymns from the late first or early second century, well after Paul's martyrdom.

How could such an advanced Christology have been understood or even exist in Paul's time? Perhaps we should interpret this portion of the letter from a different perspective. This might not actually be a hymn but might instead be the writer expressing to the Colossians what they needed to hear most: a carefully expressed refutation of the description of Christ that was being promoted by the local community, who were contending that there were other spiritual beings rivaling Christ in the salvation of the world and who were promoting a form of Gnosticism.[71]

Notice that the opening verse states: "He [Jesus Christ] is the image of the invisible God." This is an exceedingly important point that is often overlooked in our times. It states the very essence of what it is to be a true Christian. Pagans felt the need to make visible images of their gods; the God of the Christians (and Jews) was invisible. The invisible God was made visible, in human form, in Jesus Christ, who ascended into Heaven shortly after His Resurrection but

[71] Mary Ann Getty, "Colossians Reading Guide," in *The Catholic Study Bible* (Oxford: Oxford University Press, 1990).

is still present to us in the Eucharist. True Christians now consume the Body and Blood of Christ in the Eucharist, and since one becomes what one consumes, we then become visible "Christs" in the world—images of the invisible God. This is a profound reminder of the role of true Christians in the world.

The writer of this letter, without entering into debate over the existence of angelic spirits or their function, affirmed that Christ possesses the sum total of redemptive power and that the spiritual renewal of the human person occurs through contact in Baptism with the person of Christ, who died and through His divine power rose again (see Col. 2:9–14). It is, therefore, unnecessary for Christians to be concerned about placating spirits (see Col. 2:15) such as the ones who were worshipped in the local community.

Since the writer did not instruct the Colossians to separate themselves from false teachers (that is, use the ritual of excommunication to restore order in the community), we can assume that they were not faced as much with internal disorder ("unholiness") as they were with disorder coming from "outsiders" (Col. 4:5), whom we know were blending Jewish, Gnostic, and pagan ideas. As a refutation to Gnostic ideas, the writer told the Colossians that they were gifted not with "special knowledge" but with gifts of grace. Moreover, to show that Christ was above any Gnostic notions, the writer used several words in his description of the Lordship of Christ that were common to the Gnostics, such as knowledge, insight, and wisdom, but he applied them differently (see Col. 1:9–10, 28; 2:2–3; 3:10, 16; 4:5).

Such insightful counseling of the Colossians is very consistent with the character of Paul, who had committed his life to being for others what they needed most. This community was facing a threat unlike that which was in the other communities to whom Paul wrote. It's therefore reasonable to expect that he would write to them differently than in his other letters.

13.3 HOUSEHOLD NORMS

The norms of Christian family life grew out of the norms of Judaism. The Jews believed that the order in the family was under the "Master in heaven" (Col. 4:1). As noted earlier in section 10.4, in the early stages of its development, the "church" was regarded as the Household of God. Therefore, order in the "church" relied on order in the family. So the writer of this letter coached the Colossians on household norms from a hierarchical point of view, since hierarchy was an essential characteristic of order, and being orderly emulated God.[72]

In this letter, the writer spoke of wives and husbands (Col. 3:18–19), children and parents (Col. 3:20–21), and slaves and masters (Col. 3:22). Household norms are expressed in several other New Testament writings as well. Many norms reflected the circumstances of their times. The principle being taught here is that harmonious relationships depend on each person doing their part: order, not the details of order, arises from the divine creator. And so while ancient times differed from our culture in that each person's role was determined largely by culture rather than by mutual agreement, the principle of roles and harmony within relationships still holds.

13.4 SOME OTHER INSIGHTS

There does not appear to be anything in this letter to suggest that the Christian community in Colossae was recovering from a recent earthquake (60 AD), and there is no evidence of Jewish Christians having been traumatically expelled from the synagogues. It is therefore difficult to see this letter as not having been written by Paul.

[72] Fr. Raymond E. Brown, "Letter to the Colossians," in *An Introduction to the New Testament* (New Haven, CT: Yale University Press, 1997).

So the theory that Paul wrote this letter while in prison in Ephesus at about the same time that he wrote the Letter to Philemon in 55 AD holds considerable merit. But whether Colossians was written by Paul or not, this letter describes the "church" as the Body of Christ—clearly a Pauline teaching—and depicts suffering with and for the "church" as suffering by the Body of Christ.

FOURTEEN
✠ ✠ ✠
THE LETTER TO THE EPHESIANS

14.1 SOME BACKGROUND

The opening verse we normally hear from this letter is: "Paul, an apostle of Christ Jesus by the will of God, to the holy ones who are [in Ephesus] faithful in Christ Jesus" (Eph. 1:1). However, the text in brackets is not included in one of the earliest intact manuscripts we have of this letter, the Chester Beatty Papyrus II (P[46]), which is from around the year 200 AD.[73] Two early Church Fathers, Origen (ca. 250) and Basil (ca. 350), mentioned the absence of these words as well, and in two other early manuscripts, *Codex Vaticanus* (ca. 300) and *Codex Sinaiticus* (ca. 350), the text reads "in Laodicea," not "in Ephesus."[74]

Further, in Paul's letters, he usually offered greetings to named people in the community. These greetings are missing from this letter. Instead, Paul wrote that he was sending this letter with Tychicus, who was also the one entrusted to hand-carry the Letter to the Colossians (Eph. 6:21–22).

[73] Fr. Raymond E. Brown, "Letter to the Ephesians," in *An Introduction to the New Testament* (New Haven, CT: Yale University Press, 1997).

[74] "Introduction to Ephesians," in the *New American Bible, revised edition* (Washington: Confraternity of Christian Doctrine, 1986).

The text also says that "I have heard of your faith in the Lord Jesus" (Eph. 1:15, RSVCE) and "I suppose you have heard of the stewardship of God's grace that was given to me for your benefit" (Eph. 3:2). By this point, we too have to wonder: How could Paul speak so indirectly of his relations with the Ephesian community after he had spent three full years ministering there? Also, the text never refers to Jews. Instead, the listeners were addressed as "you, Gentiles in the flesh" (Eph. 2:11), even though there were many Jews in the Ephesian Christian community.

The undisputed letters of Paul were situational in character, that is, they addressed specific issues and concerns in specific communities. But as early as the seventeenth century, scholars began to see the Letter to the Ephesians not as a letter but as an encyclical—something intended to be read by a person who was journeying to many church locations. The space left blank in Ephesians 1:1 would have been filled in with the name of the city in which the document was being read.[75] This identification with Ephesians as an encyclical, however, would cause us to call into question whether this book was written by Paul, as encyclicals are thought to date from the late first century on (for example, the Book of Revelation is regarded as an encyclical).

The principal divisions in this letter are:

✠ Address (1:1–14)
✠ Unity of the Church in Christ (1:15–2:22)
✠ World Mission of the Church (3:1–4:24)
✠ Daily Conduct, an Expression of Unity (4:25–6:20)
✠ Conclusion (6:21–24)

14.2 THE CHURCH OF JESUS CHRIST

As noted earlier, for most of Paul's missionary time, the term "church" meant a federation of house-churches. But the writer of

---

[75] Brown, "Letter to the Ephesians."

this document expressed an ecclesiology (how the Church is described) that was thought, for a long time, to be beyond what was understood in Paul's lifetime.

This document deals not so much with a Christian community in the city of Ephesus but with the universal Church, the head of which is Christ (Eph. 4:15). Indeed, the writer gave a stated purpose of the universal Church — to be the instrument for making God's plan of salvation known throughout the universe (see Eph. 3:9–10).

Therefore, references to "the church" in Ephesians 1:22, 3:10, 3:21, and 5:23 clearly meant the universal Church, not just a local collection of house-churches. The text even says that the universal Church was a goal of Christ's ministry and death. This idea is supported by Jesus' own words: "And so I say to you, you are Peter, and upon this rock I will build my church" (Matt. 16:18a).

Further, the text of this letter says:

> Christ loved the church and handed himself over for her to sanctify her, cleansing her by the bath of water with the word, that he might present to himself the church in splendor, without spot or wrinkle or any such thing, that she might be holy and without blemish. (Eph. 5:25b–27)

This passage differs somewhat from Paul's other descriptions of Christ's sacrifice: in Romans 5:6, 8, he wrote that Christ died for sinners, and in 2 Corinthians 5:14–15, he wrote that Christ died for all. However, some scholars contend that Ephesians does not replace those descriptions but expands on them, making this passage the beginning of what came to be known as the "distinctive features of Catholic Christianity."[76]

---

[76] Stig Hanson, "The Unity of the Church in the New Testament: Colossians and Ephesians," *Journal of Biblical Literature* 66, no. 1 (March 1947).

14.3 ASSURANCES OF ORDER

We again need to recall that in the cultural worldview of Paul's time, order and the maintaining of order were of central importance. So the writer of Ephesians, in referring to the "church" as the Body of Christ, relied on his audience's sense of order in the body, i.e., the head rules the other parts of the body.[77] He wrote that Christians can be assured of order because in the universal Church, Christ is the "head" (see Eph. 1:22–23) over the other parts of the Body (see Eph. 4:11–12). Thus, there is an inherent order in the Church.

But the writer also said that his audience must strive to preserve that order in what is called today "the seven-fold unity of the Church": "*one body* and *one Spirit*, as you were also called to the *one hope* of your call, *one Lord, one faith, one baptism, one God and Father of all*, who is over all and through all and in all" (Eph. 4:4–6).

What is the "one baptism" referred to in this passage? Most scholars, but not all, have concluded that Baptism, which was a very public statement of one's belief in Jesus as Lord and Savior, was *the* common ritual that all Christians participated in as they passed from "darkness" (disordered life) into "light" (ordered life).[78] As we read in Ephesians 5:8–9, "For you were once darkness, but now you are light in the Lord. Live as children of light; for light produces every kind of goodness and righteousness and truth." Participating in the "one baptism" therefore brought sacred order into the life of every believer, as the ancient Jews and Christians believed that the ultimate expression of God's "holiness" (orderliness) was that God separated the light from the darkness (see Gen. 1:4b).

---

[77] Neyrey, *Paul, In Other Words: A Cultural Reading of His Letters*.

[78] Frederick F. Bruce, *The Epistles to the Colossians, to Philemon, and to the Ephesians* (Grand Rapids, MI: Eerdsmans Publishing, 1984).

Baptism not only admitted Christians into the most reliable order they could ever have, it also led them to the love of Christ for His Church, for the writer of Ephesians referred to the Church as the "bride" of Christ (see Eph. 5:21–33). Just as a Christian husband is wholly committed to his wife, and she to him, Christ is wholly committed to His Church, and the Church to Him.

As noted earlier, it is important to recognize that in expressing this assurance of order to his listeners, the writer described the Church in a very different way than did Paul in his undisputed letters. But this difference does not in itself necessarily mean that Paul didn't write this letter, because it may simply reflect a growth in his theology and understanding of ecclesiology. And so while most scholars consider Ephesians as an encyclical written in Paul's name late in the first century, a few hold that Ephesians was indeed written by Paul during his second imprisonment in Rome.[79]

14.4 SOME OTHER INSIGHTS

Paul's undisputed letters show a man struggling to help burgeoning Christian communities with concerns over:

✠ the return of Christ,
✠ Jewish Christians insisting on circumcision
and works of the law, and
✠ the ultimate fate of Christians.

Moreover, in those letters, Paul described Jesus as having been put to death for our transgressions and raised for our justification. Although most of Israel rejected Jesus, Paul proclaimed that they eventually would see Him as the true Messiah. Paul also told his

[79] Luke T. Johnson, *The Writings of the New Testament: An Interpretation* (Minneapolis: Fortress Press, 1999).

listeners that believers were united in the Risen Christ. Having been baptized into Him, they should live in anticipation of His imminent return.

But in Ephesians, it appears that most if not all of these concerns were overshadowed by new problems, especially in terms of daily conduct and growing in unity (see Eph. 4:1–6, 25–32). In particular, the writer encouraged Christians to be united in what we would term today as "spiritual warfare" with these memorable words:

> Put on the armor of God so that you may be able to stand firm against the tactics of the devil. For our struggle is not with flesh and blood but the principalities, with the powers, with the world rulers of this present darkness, with the evil spirits in the heavens Therefore, put on the armor of God, that you may be able to resist on the evil day and, having done everything, to hold your ground. So stand fast with your loins girded in truth, clothed with righteousness as a breastplate, and your feet shod in readiness for the gospel of peace. In all circumstances, hold faith as a shield, to quench all [the] flaming arrows of the evil one. And take the helmet of salvation and the sword of the Spirit, which is the word of God. (Eph 6:11-17)

In promoting unity in the community, he writer urges his audience: We, the Body of Christ (the universal Church), are all together in this. Christ is with us; He has given us the Church as the vessel in which we are to journey together, through both good and bad times. Of course, this applies not just in Ephesus but in all Christian communities.

FIFTEEN

✠ ✠ ✠

THE SECOND LETTER TO
THE THESSALONIANS

15.1 SOME BACKGROUND

In 1903, William Wrede, a leading German theologian of the late nineteenth century, presented arguments against the tradition that Paul wrote 2 Thessalonians.[80] For the most part, his arguments rested on linguistics. For example, the sentence structure in 2 Thessalonians is quite different from that in 1 Thessalonians. 2 Thessalonians is also much more formal in tone than 1 Thessalonians, and the vocabulary of 2 Thessalonians is much closer to Colossians and Ephesians. Nevertheless, there are still greater similarities between 1 Thessalonians and 2 Thessalonians than there are between any of Paul's undisputed letters, and there are even entire sections from 1 Thessalonians that are repeated verbatim in 2 Thessalonians. These similarities, however, cause us to question: Why would Paul copy himself in such a mechanical way? Is this copying not evidence of one assuming the mantle of Paul in writing 2 Thessalonians?

---

[80] William Wrede, *The Authenticity of the Second Letter to the Thessalonians Investigated*, trans. Robert Rhea (1903; repr., Cambridge, UK: James Clarke and Co., 2018).

This letter closes with: "This greeting is in my own hand, Paul's. This is the sign in every letter; this is how I write" (2 Thess. 3:17). But the writer here may have been insisting on the genuineness of his letter and not necessarily on the idea that Paul himself was actually writing. Or he could be setting this letter apart from other "forged" Pauline letters (see 2 Thess. 2:2), which might suggest that 2 Thessalonians was written sometime after Paul's death.

In the midst of this puzzle, there are a few passages and clues that may help us date this letter. In 2 Thessalonians 2:4, for example, this letter refers to the "temple of God." Does this imply that the letter was written when the Temple in Jerusalem was still standing, or does "temple" here refer to the universal Church?[81] The first understanding would allow for a Pauline authorship, but the second could not help us determine the date of this letter, since anyone at any time could have used the word "temple" to mean the Church.

2 Thessalonians has apocalyptic imagery similar to what we find in the Book of Revelation, which was written near the end of the first century. The early Christians understood Evil as working on a global scale against God, and so they turned to the Jewish apocalyptic images to make sense of their world.[82] Much of that Jewish apocalyptic imagery was shaped by the Book of Daniel. The apocalyptic genre, however, was common in Jewish literature from about 200 BC to 100 AD, however, so this apocalyptic imagery cannot help us narrow the timing of the letter's authorship.

In terms of the culture and geography of Thessalonica, as was noted earlier, it was not only the largest city in what was then

---

[81] Footnote to 2 Thessalonians 2:4 in the *New American Bible, revised edition* (Washington: Confraternity of Christian Doctrine, 1970).

[82] Fr. Raymond E. Brown, "Second Letter to the Thessalonians," in *An Introduction to the New Testament* (New Haven, CT: Yale University Press, 1997).

Macedonia, but it was also a chief location on the Via Egnatia, the main Roman trade road that led into Byzantium (later known as Constantinople) — a distance of nearly 700 miles. The city is located where the Axios River flows into the Aegean Sea, and so people coming along the river from the interior of what is now Bulgaria, people traveling over land along the Via Egnatia, and people traveling by sea all (out of necessity) had to pass through Thessalonica. Although the city was originally Greek, by the first century it was distinctly Roman in character, having a large amphitheater for gladiatorial games, Roman baths, and a massive two-terraced forum.[83]

The principal divisions in this letter are:

✠ Address (1:1–12)
✠ Warning About Deception Concerning the *Parousia* (2:1–12)
✠ Thanksgiving and Prayer (2:13–17)
✠ Ethical Exhortation (3:1–16)
✠ Conclusion (3:17–18)

15.2 MESSAGE OF HOPE

This letter speaks to a people who were enduring *thlipsis*, which is translated as "tribulations" (2 Thess. 1:4). The tribulations were seen by Christians as a necessary prelude to Christ's return. The writer went on to say, however: do not "be shaken out of your minds suddenly, or to be alarmed either by a 'spirit,' or by an oral statement, or by a letter allegedly from us to the effect that the day of the Lord is at hand" (2 Thess. 2:2). The "Day of the Lord"

[83] *Joseph Roisman and Ian Worthington, A Companion to Ancient Macedonia (New York: John Wiley, 2011).*

was a term used to refer to Jesus' Second Coming, and it's evident from this passage that false teachers, perhaps in Paul's name (which would account for the concern over forged letters), were claiming that Christ had already returned.[84]

But the writer told the Thessalonians that much would take place before Jesus returns: "unless the apostasy comes first and the lawless one is revealed" (2 Thess. 2:3b). Therefore, do not be alarmed, for any trials or tribulations are part of God's plan. The "apostasy" must take place and "the lawless one" must be revealed for what he is (an agent of the devil), because "the mystery of lawlessness is already at work" (2 Thess. 2:7a).

"Lawlessness" was a rejection of authority—God's authority. Behind the "mystery of lawlessness" was the Evil One, Satan. The writer said, however, that Christ was restraining "the lawless one" (see 2 Thess. 2:7b) until the divine plan for proclaiming the gospel to all the world had been accomplished.[85] The writer then described in apocalyptic terms how Jesus would triumph over "the lawless one" (see 2 Thess. 2:8–10). And so he ended this section with a promise of hope to the people in the midst of their tribulations.

15.3 COMFORT IN ORDER

There was great comfort to be found in Jesus being in control, but there was also great comfort in order itself. Remember that to first-century Jews and Christians, to be orderly was to be holy. So the writer concluded this letter by invoking his audience's sense of comfort in order. He reminded them that everyone has his or her part and that everyone must do that part to sustain order. The time of waiting

---

[84]   Fr. Raymond E. Brown, *An Introduction to New Testament Christology* (Mahwah, NJ: Paulist Press, 1994).

[85]   Joulette M. Bassler, "The Enigmatic Sign: 2 Thessalonians 1:5," *Catholic Biblical Quarterly* 46, no. 3 (July 1984).

for Jesus' return may be longer than expected, but we must maintain hope and order. Those who were idle, who did not do their part, threatened the order in the community (see 2 Thess. 3:6–15).

15.4 SOME OTHER INSIGHTS

It's fairly evident that this letter offered hope and encouragement to a people under intense pressure. The Thessalonians were experiencing tribulations, cultural struggles, and false teachings. But the writer of this letter promised them hope in the midst of their struggles, a hope that we, too, can maintain today as we await the Second Coming of Christ.

SIXTEEN
✠ ✠ ✠

CLOSING THOUGHTS

We began this guide to Paul and his letters with the statement that there is a treasure trove of insights in St. Paul's letters, insights into the life, death, and Resurrection of Jesus Christ and advice on how to live out the life of self-emptying to which Jesus calls each of us. We have investigated Paul and his letters through the cultural world-view of his time, and we have learned that the people of the first century AD valued order and community and that they lived in a very non-individualistic world. By viewing the words, imagery, and language of Paul's letters in light of the times and culture in which they were written, we have been able to understand his writings better than we had been before.

Throughout his life, Paul maintained his loyalty to the essentials of Jewish faith: belief in the one true God and zealousness for the Law (the Ten Commandments). And so Paul helped to develop Christian terminology by using terms that had roots in Judaism and Koine Greek. Paul's letters have given us much of the vocabulary of Christianity that we have become familiar with: he was the first to give a Christian meaning to "grace," "apostle," and "gospel." The communities to which he wrote revered his writings and sought to preserve them and share them with neighboring communities.

Because Paul, a first-century Eastern Mediterranean, viewed the world as highly organized by God's plan, everything was to be in its proper place. He classified people and things in very dualistic terms such as "in" or "out," "clean" or "unclean," and so on. He viewed the physical body in the same way as he viewed the social body and the church body—intended as orderly organisms. But as his knowledge and trust in Christ grew, he formulated new "classifications," new "boundaries," and new "structures" to express order and proper place in a Christ-centered cosmos. We see from his letters that Paul was deeply worried about the attacks of Satan (the Evil One) and his agents who were threatening to destroy what was good and godly in Christ's Church. Paul was sensitive to persons and things that crossed "proper" boundary lines and was concerned with the rituals associated with restoring and maintaining those boundaries: sin was not only a violation of rules but a corrupting and polluting influence on the whole community. This need for order in the community explains why Paul advocated so strongly for the ritual of excommunication in many of his letters.

In chapter 1, as we were preparing to enter into Paul's letters, we noted that the larger world around Christians perceived Christianity as threatening, because it brings with it a symbolic universe, or social worldview, one that is substantially at odds with the prevailing non-Christian worldview. This "divide" between Christians and the world around them manifested itself in the life circumstances of many of Paul's first listeners. This divide, and the troubles that attend it, are close to the heart of what Paul writes in his letters.

What we are painfully aware of in our times is that this "divide" persists to this day. Christian values and norms of conduct are as much at odds with the prevailing non-Christian worldview of our time as they were in Paul's. But it goes much deeper than disagreements over matters of principle. There is indeed a cosmic struggle going on between God and the Devil. Christians are, entangled in that spiritual warfare and will be until the day of Jesus' return. The advice offered to the Ephesians is as timely now as it was then, and it bears repeating:

> Put on the armor of God so that you may be able to stand firm against the tactics of the devil. For our struggle is not with flesh and blood but the principalities, with the powers, with the world rulers of this present darkness, with the evil spirits in the heavens Therefore, put on the armor of God, that you may be able to resist on the evil day and, having done everything, to hold your ground. So stand fast with your loins girded in truth, clothed with righteousness as a breastplate, and your feet shod in readiness for the gospel of peace. In all circumstances, hold faith as a shield, to quench all [the] flaming arrows of the evil one. And take the helmet of salvation and the sword of the Spirit, which is the word of God. (Eph 6:11-17)

From the very beginning, Christians are "in" this world but are not "of" this world.

Clearly, Paul was called for a mission, and he took it on with everything he had. He was not "in it" for the popularity or the power or the money. Paul risked his life every day because the good news he had received was so good that he felt compelled to share it with everyone he could. He believed in it deeply, and he sought to bring others to that same conviction.

We have sought here, in this brief guide to Paul's theology and letters, to "hear" his words of counsel in a different light than we may have encountered before. We have been deliberately more cognizant of the anthropological setting of Paul's words and of the fact that while we delve more deeply into his writings, we are still reading inspired Sacred Scripture. Our purpose in this investigation has been simple: discerning what Paul's words meant in the times in which they were written is an important steppingstone to discerning the timeless message that God intends for us even today.

BIBLIOGRAPHY

Allies, Mary H. *The Best of Augustine: Selections from the Writings of St Augustine of Hippo.* London: Burns and Oates, 2016.

Alter, Robert. *The Art of Biblical Narrative.* New York: Basic Books, 2011.

"Apostasia." In Strong's Exhaustive Concordance. Peabody, MA: Hendrickson Publishers, 2009.

Baugh, Steve M. "A Foreign World: Ephesus in the First Century." In *Women in the Church.* Wheaton, IL: Crossway Publishers, 2005.

Bassler, Joulette M. "The Enigmatic Sign: 2 Thessalonians 1:5." *Catholic Biblical Quarterly* 46, no. 3 (July 1984).

Berger, Peter and Thomas Luckmann. *The Social Construction of Reality.* New York: Anchor Books, 1966.

Bibliowicz, Abel M. *Jewish-Christian Relations: The First Centuries.* WA: Mascarat Publishing, 2019.

Boswell, J. E., "Exposition and Oblation: The Abandonment of Children and the Ancient and Medieval Family." In *American Historical Review.* Oxford: Oxford University Press, 1984.

Brown, Fr. Raymond E. *An Introduction to New Testament Christology.* Mahwah, NJ: Paulist Press, 1994.

———. *An Introduction to the New Testament.* New Haven, CT: Yale University Press, 1997.

———. *The Death of the Messiah.* Vol. 2. New Haven, CT: Yale University Press, 1994.

Bruce, Frederick F. *New Testament History.* New York: Galilee Doubleday, 1980.

————. *The Epistles to the Colossians, to Philemon, and to the Ephesians*. Grand Rapids, MI: Eerdsmans Publishing, 1984.

Carson, Donald A. and Douglas Moo. *An Introduction to the New Testament*. Grand Rapids, MI: Zondervan Academic, 2005.

"Codex Vaticanus." In *Catholic Encyclopedia*. Nashville, TN: Thomas Nelson Inc., 1990.

Cuddy, Chris and Mark Hart. *Sword of the Spirit: A Beginner's Guide to St. Paul*. Mesa, AZ: Life Teen Inc., 2008.

Danker, Frederick William. "Ioudaios." In *A Greek-English Lexicon of the New Testament and Other Early Christian Literature*. Chicago: University of Chicago Press, 2009.

Deissmann, Gustav Adolf. *Light from the Ancient East*. London: Hodder and Stoughton, 1910.

Douglas, Mary T. *Natural Symbols*. London: Routledge Classics, 1996.

Fantham, Elaine et. al. Women in the Classical World. Oxford: Oxford University Press, 1994.

Fromer, Margaret and Shar Keyes. *Letters to the Thessalonians*. Wheaton, IL: Harold Shaw Publishers, 1975.

Futrell, Alison. *Blood in the Arena: The Spectacle of Roman Power*. Austin, TX: University of Texas Press, 1997.

Getty, Mary Ann. "Colossians Reading Guide." In *The Catholic Study Bible*. Oxford: Oxford University Press, 1990.

————. *Paul and His Writings*. Oxford: Oxford University Press, 1990.

Hahn, Scott. *Catholic Commentary on Sacred Scripture: Romans*. Grand Rapids, MI: Baker Academic, 2017.

Hanson, Stig. "The Unity of the Church in the New Testament: Colossians and Ephesians." *Journal of Biblical Literature* 66, no. 1 (March 1947).

Hoklotubbe, T. Christopher, *Civilized Piety: The Rhetoric of Pietas in the Pastoral Epistles and the Roman Empire*, Waco, Texas: Baylor University Press, 2017.

Holloway, Carl R. "The Pauline Letters." In *A Critical Introduction to the New Testament*. Nashville, TN: Abingdon Press, 2005.

Johnson, Luke T. *The Writings of the New Testament: An Interpretation.* Minneapolis: Fortress Press, 1999.

Lightfoot, Joseph Barber. *Notes on the Epistles of St. Paul.* 1895. Reprint, London: Forgotten Books, 2018.

Magris, Aldo. "Gnosticism from Its Origins to the Middle Ages." In *MacMillan Encyclopedia of Religion.* 2005.

Matthews, Victor and Don Benjamin. *Social World of Ancient Israel.* Peabody, MA: Hendrickson Publishers, 1993.

Marrow, Fr. Stanley B. *Paul: His Letters and His Theology.* Mahwah, NJ: Paulist Press, 1986.

Monks of St. Augustine Abbey. The Book of Saints. London: Adam and Charles Black, 1966.

Mott, Stephen Charles. "Greek Ethics and Christian Conversion: The Philonic Background of Titus." *New Testament* 20, no. 1 (January 1978).

Mounce, William D. *Basics of Biblical Greek.* Grand Rapids, MI: Zondervan, 2003.

Murphy-O'Conner, Jerome. *Paul the Letter-Writer: His World, His Opinions, His Skills.* Collegeville, MN: Liturgical Press, 1995.

———. "II Timothy Contrasted with I Timothy and Titus." *Biblical Review* 98 (1991).

The Navarre Bible: Thessalonians and Pastoral Letters. Dublin: Four Courts Press, 1992.

Neyrey, Jerome H. *Paul, In Other Words: A Cultural Reading of His Letters.* Louisville, KY: John Knox Press, 1990.

Pherigo, Lindsey P. "Paul's Life after the Close of Acts." *Journal of Biblical Literature* 70, no. 4 (December 1951): 277ff.

Pope, Hugh. "Kingdom of God." In *The Catholic Encyclopedia.* New York: Robert Appleton Company, 1910.

Roisman, Joseph and Ian Worthington. A Companion to Ancient Macedonia. New York: John Wiley, 2011.

Senior, Fr. Donald et al., eds. "Reading Guide to 1 Corinthians." In *The Catholic Study Bible.* Oxford: Oxford University Press, 1990.

"Slavery in the Roman World." In *Ancient History Encyclopedia*. Horsham, UK: World History Encyclopedia Ltd., 2013.

Wills, Garry. *What Paul Meant*. New York: Penguin Books, 2006.

Witherington III, Ben. *A Week in the Life of Corinth*. Westmont, IL: Inter-Varsity Press, 2012.

Wrede, William. *The Authenticity of the Second Letter to the Thessalonians Investigated*. Translated by Robert Rhea. 1903. Reprint, Cambridge, UK: James Clarke and Co., 2018.

GLOSSARY OF TERMS
(AS THEY WERE USED IN THE FIRST CENTURY)

Adoption
In the ancient Middle East, every child needed to be adopted, in a sense. When a child was born, the infant was not part of the family until a male (biological father or not) claimed the child as his own and gave the infant a name. At that point, the male became the infant's father and accepted full care and responsibility for the child's survival.

Apostle
Initially, the Koine Greek word *apóstolos* (translated as "apostle") meant "one who is sent." The Hebrew word was *shaliah*, which implied an emissary sent to represent another. Paul used the word "apostle" to refer to anyone, including himself, who was sent by Christ to proclaim the gospel ("good news") of salvation through Jesus Christ. Later, Luke said in his Gospel that Jesus sent out the Twelve "whom he also named apostles" (Luke 6:13). So in some quarters, the term was limited to the chosen Twelve (and also Mathias, who replaced Judas).

Author
In the ancient world, the person whose authority is behind a written work, not necessarily the "writer" of that work. The "writer" often did not actually *write* the work but rather dictated it to a *grammateus*, or "scribe."

Body

In the Greco-Roman view, the *soma* (body), *psyche* (soul), and *pneuma* (spirit) made up the human person, whose physical structure was *sarx*, usually translated as "flesh." *Sarx* also meant the human body. The human body had hierarchical order, the head being the most important and the feet being the least. What entered through the sense of sight was more important than what entered through the sense of touch, and so on. The more bodily behaviors were controlled, the more orderly society would be. All bodily disorder, including illness and injury, was regarded as resulting from a failure to control one's body. Just as a community's boundaries could be threatened, so a body's boundaries could be threatened. So there was great concern over what entered and left the body. An "unholy" body, i.e., one that was not under control, could not come into the presence of God. Any contact with the bodily fluids of another person made someone "unholy" because the fluids were not "in their proper place." In addition, a body that was not complete or was deformed in some way was not "holy" because it did not exhibit proper order.

Breaking of the Bread

This was the term used by early Christians for what is known today as the Eucharist.

Church

The Koine Greek word *ekklesia* (translated as "church") meant "a called community." The approximate Hebrew term was *qahal Yahweh*, which meant "household of God." In the letters attributed to Paul, *ekklesia*, "church," was used in two ways:

A federation of house-churches in a city or geographic area. The church in Corinth and the church in Ephesus are examples. Prior to the destruction of the Temple in 70 AD, Christians first went to synagogue services and then to house-churches (private homes) for the Breaking of the Bread (Eucharist), which was presided over by a presbyter who was often assisted by at least one deacon. Paul appointed bishops and presbyters to provide cohesion to each federation of house-churches.

Later, the use of *ekklesia* ("church") in letters attributed to Paul meant the entire called community of believers, which he also referred to as "the Body of Christ" because they partook of the Body of Christ in the Eucharist.

Creation

In the first century, Creation was regarded as the ultimate expression of God's orderliness. To be orderly was to be holy, as God is holy. They saw God's holiness as observable in the order of nature. God gave man dominion over His ordered creation to keep things orderly. (Note: today, Creation is seen as an expression of God's love and desire to share that love with creatures.)

Curse of the Law

This term was used by Paul to observe that prior to Christ's salvific act, people were required to observe "the law," yet they could have no access to eternal life.

Day of the Lord

Initially, the Jews used this term to mean the time when the Lord would come and vindicate His people. Christians later used the term in referring to Jesus' Second Coming (the *Parousia*).

Diatribe

In the ancient world, a diatribe was a discourse that raised hypothetical questions and then responded to them, or the speaker or writer stated false conclusions and then went on to refute them. There was a great deal of subtlety to diatribe. Sometimes the refutation offered didn't actually answer the hypothetical question raised but instead spoke to the "real" issue the speaker or writer was addressing. (Note: today, diatribe implies a forceful and bitter verbal attack against someone or something and is regarded as hostile.)

Good vs. Evil

In the first century, the conflict between Good and Evil was seen as playing out on a cosmic scale. The early Christians envisioned a cosmic duel going on between Good and Evil, who were seen as personified beings—one an agent of God, the other an enemy of God—who both had influence over mankind. They envisioned a whole army of enemies of God at work in the world: death, rulers, tempters, demons, Rome, evil spirits, and the power of darkness, just to name a few. Even Sin was seen as a personified force opposing God.

Grace

Initially, the Koine Greek word *charis* meant "favor." Paul sought a word for the undeserved divine nourishment, or sanctification, promised by Jesus, the gift resulting from the death of Christ: renewed access to eternal life. So he used *charis* (translated as "grace"), since there was no word for divine nourishment in Koine Greek. Hebrews had long thought of *charis* as God's favor to them for their living virtuous lives. (Note: the more formal meaning today is that which brings about or sustains holiness in us and which aids us in particular actions in our life (see *CCC* 1996–2005).)

Greeks

Jews used the Koine Greek word *hellenes* (usually translated as "the Greeks") to refer to Gentiles in general, not just the Greek people.

Gospel

The Koine Greek word *evangelio* (usually translated as "gospel") meant "good news." Paul used the term to mean the "good news" of Jesus Christ: that mankind has been redeemed (brought back to where we belong, with access to eternal life with God) through Jesus' Passion and death, not through anything we have done.

Hang on a Tree

During the Roman Era, the term meant to crucify. The body of a crucified criminal was regarded by Jews as "cursed" in that it could defile the whole land if not immediately buried.

He'tot

A ritual presided over by a Temple priest that involved an animal sacrifice and that marked a person's transition from being defiled or "unclean" to being "clean," restoring the person to proper order in their life and the community.

Honor

"Honor" in the ancient Middle East did not have to do with one's personal integrity; it was the esteem others held you in. Personal identity was group-centered: one's worth was defined by the "witness" of those around them, not by one's character or deeds. Honor was the highest "virtue," transcending all others.

Jewish Myths

In Paul's letters, this term referred to what came to be known in the second century as Gnosticism, from the Greek word *gnosis* (usually translated as "knowledge"), which had its early roots in Judaism. Gnostics claimed that the principal element of salvation came from special knowledge of the supreme divinity in the form of mystical insights that only Gnostics had. In Gnosticism, there were no concepts of sin and repentance; rather, it was all about enlightenment.

Justification (Righteousness)

The Koine Greek word *dikaiosyne* (often translated as "justification" or "righteousness") meant to be delivered from a deserved punishment. The Hebrew word *tzedakah*, which was translated as *dikaiosyne* in the Septuagint, meant to hold justice and mercy in right balance, as God does. This is also the meaning of righteousness that generally applies throughout Scripture. However, Paul used *dikaiosyne* to mean one's being in right balance with God. It cannot be earned but must be actively and continually accepted. Paul's use of one term to mean two different things (justification or righteousness) has confused many listeners and readers. (Note: people today think of "righteousness" as an ongoing state in life, whereas being "justified," or having "justification," as happening in a single event. But this is not the understanding that Paul intended.)

Jews

The Koine Greek word *ioudaioi* (usually translated as "the Jews") was the term used for the Jewish authorities: both civil and religious authorities were the same. The Jewish people themselves were referred to as *israēlítēi* ("Israelites").

Kingdom of God	Paul used the term *basileian theou* (usually translated as "kingdom of God") to mean Heaven, which differs from the meaning of that term in the Gospels. (Note: the formal meaning today is: "A way of living in which Christ reigns in the hearts of believers as they strive to fulfill the will of God in this life. It separates us from the kingdom of the world and the devil."[1])
The Law	Paul used the Koine Greek word *nomos* (usually translated as "the law") to have two meanings: The Decalogue (the Ten Commandments). Observing the Decalogue is mankind's way of accepting the freely-given gift of salvation. The Mosaic Law (the *mitzvot* or "commandments") defining the terms of loyalty to God. The rituals of *mitzvot* were regarded as making the "observer" more pleasing to God as he or she ensured divine help and protection. In reading Paul's letters, one has to infer from the context which meaning was intended.
Misfortune	In the first century, misfortune was seen as the working of malevolent forces, agents of Evil. And misfortune could only be dealt with through appeasing those evil forces in the world. Even dying was seen as a misfortune caused by the power of Death working through malevolent forces.
Order	In the first century, order was regarded as the emulation of God. The people believed that they had to keep everything in its proper place and separate what did not belong together. Each person "had their proper place": male/female, child/adult, slave/freeman, Jew/Gentile, etc. God expressed His holiness by creating an orderly universe with a proper structure of relationships, and so the maintaining of order was of central importance. The Final Judgment was seen as the time of ultimate orderliness.

---

[1] Pope, "Kingdom of God."

Pietas

Latin for "loyalty." To Romans, *pietas* was their solemn duty "to the gods, to country and to family." It was even touted on some of their coins. But to Middle Easterners, *pietas* had a much deeper more personal meaning. It did not relate to "the gods" or to "country" but rather it was the profound responsibility each person had for the care and guidance of each member of their extended family. In the ancient Middle East, family came before all else. In their communities, there were no social services, no police force. Each extended family was responsible for the well-being and proper conduct of its members and the larger community relied on them to meet that responsibility. There was also no social security system; each extended family was responsible for caring for its members, even those who no longer lived at home.

Presbyter

Initially, the Koine Greek word *presbyteros* meant an elder male. In the early Christian era, it was used to mean the head-of-household who presided over the Breaking of the Bread. This is the origins of the Christian priesthood.

Resurrection

In the first century, the Jewish view was that "the resurrection" would involve a restoration of the nation of Israel, not of each individual person. Some people would benefit from the fact that the resurrection took place, but there was no common agreement on how they would benefit. Paul, however, taught that there would be individual bodily resurrection into eternal life for each human being, because Christ Himself was bodily resurrected into eternal life. Christ was the first born of the dead among many brothers (see Col. 1:18 and Rom. 8:29).

Righteousness

See Justification.

Salvation

The Koine Greek word *sotiria* meant to be saved from some impending danger. In Greek mythology, Sotiria was the goddess of safety and salvation. Among Jews, salvation was understood to mean being saved from oppression by others, such as the Romans. But Paul taught that *sotiria* (translated as "salvation") was being saved from the gravest consequence of sin: spiritual death (having no access to eternal life). This salvation was won for us by the death of Christ on the Cross. The idea of sharing eternal life with God was unimaginable to Jews.

Satan

For many centuries, Satan (also known as the devil) was seen as the "accuser of the people before God." That is, Satan was an adversary of God's people, not an adversary of God. However, in the first century AD, Christians began to see Satan and the Evil One as being one and the same being. In time, the personified being Sin was also seen as being the Evil One, the adversary of God.

Self-emptying

Freeing oneself from personal or selfish concerns.

Servant

Among Gentiles, a servant was a domestic worker in the household. However, among Hebrews, a servant was a debt-slave. It was unlawful for a Hebrew to enslave another Hebrew, so they referred to debt-slaves as "servants." In the ancient Mediterranean, the most common reasons for incurring debt were crop failure and the inability to pay taxes, which were an enormous economic burden under the Roman Empire. A wealthy neighbor would loan a poorer neighbor the money to pay his taxes, but the loan was secured by the debtor's land and the labor of the members of the debtor's household. When a household defaulted, which happened very often, the creditor foreclosed on the land, and those in the debtor's household became "indentured," or debt-slaves, to the creditor. These "servants" were marked by a symbol of shame: large earrings or tags of ownership (see Exod. 21:6).

Sin Initially, "Sin" was seen as a personified being who had power over human beings and who caused them to be out of "proper order" in their lives. The personification of Sin gave ancient people an "acceptable" reason for their sinful condition. In time, however, sin came to be seen not as a personified being but as the breaking of one's relationship with God, which arises out of the disposition of one's heart. In this view, each person had a personal responsibility for their sinful behavior.

Suffering For many centuries, suffering was seen as punishment for being disorderly ("unholy") or for being out of proper order. Suffering could only be alleviated by restoring order. Much of the work of ancient "physicians" was to engage in rituals that sought to restore order in the one who was suffering. Christianity brought a different understanding to suffering. Suffering is an unfortunate occurrence that, when accepted with grace, shares in the salvific act of Jesus Christ.

Redemption The Koine Greek word *exagora* meant to be returned to one's proper place or to be restored to one's former prosperity. To Jews in the Babylonian Captivity, it meant to be returned to the Promised Land. But after their return, it came to mean that they would be restored to the prosperity of the Davidic Kingdom. By the first century AD, "redemption" referred to buying the freedom of debt-slaves. Paul used the Koine Greek word *soter*, which is usually translated as "Savior," rather than *lytrotes*, which is usually translated as "Redeemer" (see Rom. 1:16; 11:11; 13:11), to distance his listeners from their present understanding of redemption. Paul taught that *exagora* (translated as "redemption") was mankind being brought back to where they belonged: namely, sharing eternal life with God and being restored to the prosperity of adopted children of God, heirs through Jesus Christ.

Rituals	In the ancient word, rituals were fastidiously performed rites that were needed to expel the ill that had permeated a person's life. These rituals thereby restored and maintained proper order. A ritual marked a transition from one's present state to a more ordered state. Because maintaining proper order was central to the ancient people's sustained existence and their seeking godliness, their lives were steeped in rituals that sought to restore and maintain life in its proper order.
the Spirit (later "Holy Spirit")	The term initially meant the animating and empowering force that baptized Christians received. This was later thought to be a manifestation of God, and still later, the Third Person of the Blessed Trinity.
Traditions of Our Ancestors (or the Elders)	Among Jews, this phrase meant the many unwritten "laws" that governed proper conduct.
Wisdom	The Koine Greek word *sophia* is typically translated as "wisdom." Throughout much of the Old Testament, wisdom referred to the knowledge of the order of nature. Since the ancient Jews saw God manifested in the order of nature, wisdom, then, would lead to knowledge of God. By the first century, the meaning of wisdom had broadened to knowledge demonstrated in achieving an end. For many centuries, Paul's use of *sophia* in 1 Corinthians has been interpreted as Paul explaining how Christ's death on the Cross was God's plan of salvation (see 1 Cor. 2:6–3:4).
Witchcraft	In the ancient world, witchcraft was the practice of invoking spirits (the forces of Evil) to gain an advantage over others. By invoking the enemies of God, those who practiced witchcraft were considered enemies of the people. To be a victim of witchcraft was considered to be the ultimate misfortune.
Works of the Law	Paul used this phrase to mean the rituals of *mitzvot*, observing the Mosaic Law.

Index of Names & Subjects

Vicarious Satisfaction, 50–51

W

witchcraft, 168

Z

Zoroastrianism, 90

About the Author

Deacon Bob Evans and his wife, Rose, live in Phoenix, Arizona. He serves as a deacon in the Roman Catholic Diocese of Phoenix, ministering at Blessed Sacrament Parish in Scottsdale. They have three children and six grandchildren. His formal training in Scripture was at the Kino Institute. Since 2004, he has been engaged in extensive biblical studies, and he is a popular teacher who draws heavily from the works of many others in bringing people deeper into Sacred Scripture. He regularly teaches on St. Paul's letters, biblical foundations, Scripture for homiletics, and Jesus' parables in a diaconate post-ordination program. He serves the Diocese of Phoenix as the Assistant Director of Deacon Personnel. His blog posts can be found at https://www.stephensbrother.com/, and he is the author of the recent award-winning text, *Walking the Parables of Jesus.*

Sophia Institute

Sophia Institute is a nonprofit institution that seeks to nurture the spiritual, moral, and cultural life of souls and to spread the gospel of Christ in conformity with the authentic teachings of the Roman Catholic Church.

Sophia Institute Press fulfills this mission by offering translations, reprints, and new publications that afford readers a rich source of the enduring wisdom of mankind.

Sophia Institute also operates the popular online resource CatholicExchange.com. *Catholic Exchange* provides world news from a Catholic perspective as well as daily devotionals and articles that will help readers to grow in holiness and live a life consistent with the teachings of the Church.

In 2013, Sophia Institute launched Sophia Institute for Teachers to renew and rebuild Catholic culture through service to Catholic education. With the goal of nurturing the spiritual, moral, and cultural life of souls, and an abiding respect for the role and work of teachers, we strive to provide materials and programs that are at once enlightening to the mind and ennobling to the heart; faithful and complete, as well as useful and practical.

Sophia Institute gratefully recognizes the Solidarity Association for preserving and encouraging the growth of our apostolate over the course of many years. Without their generous and timely support, this book would not be in your hands.

www.SophiaInstitute.com
www.CatholicExchange.com
www.SophiaInstituteforTeachers.org

Sophia Institute Press is a registered trademark of Sophia Institute.
Sophia Institute is a tax-exempt institution as defined by the
Internal Revenue Code, Section 501(c)(3). Tax ID 22-2548708.